Thank you for the Wi

Ending Lateral Violence

Creating Emotionally and Physically Safe Workplaces

Jill Weisensel, M.S.

LIVE LEFT OF BANG!

Truths Publishing
Milwaukee, WI

www.EndingLateralViolence.com

For bulk-purchasing pricing, please contact:
  Vistelar, LLC
  1845 N. Farwell Ave., Suite 210
  Milwaukee, WI 53202
  Phone: 877-690-8230
  Fax: 866-406-2374
  Email: info@vistelar.com
  Web: www.vistelar.com

Weisensel, Jill
Ending Lateral Violence / Jill Weisensel
First Edition 2022

ISDN 13: 978-1-7323768-1-6
ISDN 10: 1-7323768-1-6

LCCN: 2022944802

BISAC Subject Headings:
  EDUCATION / Violence & Harassment
  SELF-HELP / Communications & Social Skills
  SELF-HELP / Safety & Security / Personal Safety & Self-Defense

Published By Truths Publishing, Milwaukee, WI
Printed In the United States of America

Table of Contents

Part Three: Best Practices and Next Steps for Taking Action

Introduction

Ending Lateral Violence: Creating Emotionally and Physically Safe Workplaces offers strategies and skills that organizations can implement system-wide to address workplace toxicity. It also describes concrete steps individuals can take immediately to create safer environments that are incompatible with antisocial and aggressive behavior.

According to a recent article published in the MIT Sloan Management Review, approximately 24 million Americans left their jobs between April and September of 2021. Researchers Donald Sull, Charles Sull, and Ben Zweig analyzed millions of these employee profiles to determine the cause of the mass exodus and the exact cause of what is driving people out the door.

Do you know what they found? That "a toxic corporate culture is by far the strongest predictor of industry-adjusted attrition and is ten times more important than compensation in predicting turnover." (Sull, Sull & Zweig, 2021)

Furthermore, their analysis found that "the leading elements contributing to toxic workplace cultures included the failure to promote diversity, equity and inclusion; workers feeling disrespected; and unethical behavior." (Sull et al., 2021)

It is unacceptable to allow the epidemic of workplace violence and environmentally toxic behaviors to continue.

It is unacceptable to allow the epidemic of workplace violence and environmentally toxic behaviors to continue.

With that being said, the research is crystal clear that your workplace culture (whether healthy or unhealthy) will have a direct impact on both your quality of work and your overall quality of life. Being exposed to a toxic workplace culture over time has been linked to severe adverse health outcomes including chronic fatigue, depression, heart and lung disease, and cancer.

The information and methods included in this book were developed to help create a workplace environment that is both respectful and emotionally and physically safer. Everyone within an organization will find value in the content covered throughout the book—because we all have a role to play in creating an environment that is incompatible with emotional and physical violence.

This book will teach you how to recognize, prevent, and mitigate workplace violence (violence or the threat of violence against workers) and, if such violence occurs, how to safely respond and recover. It is my sincere hope that this book will help you in living a happier, healthier, and safer life - both at work and at home. The focus of this book will be on lateral violence (non-physical, but harmful, behavior between members of a community) but, as you will see, any discussion of lateral violence must include the broader issue of workplace violence.

This book was specifically designed as a go-to resource for strategies and high-impact solutions. Unlike other non-fiction books you've read, this book was not written in the typical "here is a story and now here is the teaching point" fashion.

Instead, since the problem of lateral violence is so damaging and so pervasive, I wrote the book with the assumption that readers will have their own personal stories, examples, and situations that will resonate and have a far greater impact than any particular story I could share. As you read through the book, I encourage you to think about how the learning points apply to your personal experiences.

For that reason, I structured the contents of the book differently than you might expect. The first part of the book takes a deep dive into the research that proves the dangerous personal and professional costs of letting lateral violence go unchecked. This part frames the problem and explains the "what and the why."

The second part of the book outlines some of the theories and strategies that can be put in place both personally and organizationally to end the problem. This part explains "who" can do something about it.

And finally, the third part of the book explains the methods and skills that you can use to achieve the goal of ending lateral violence and creating a healthy workplace environment. This part explains "how" you can end the problem, and how you can do it safely.

Each chapter starts by summarizing points from the previous chapter and ends with a list of actionable and key takeaways, to help you quickly pick up where you left off, or to help you quickly recognize the next steps for taking action.

The content of this book has been in development for many years. After finishing my first book in 2014 (Confidence in Conflict for Campus Life) that touched on the problem of lateral violence at the college and university level, I knew I wanted to dig deeper into this topic in a subsequent book. I was still working full time at Marquette University in Milwaukee, WI so this meant spending much of my off time researching, reading the relevant work of subject matter experts from around the world, and speaking with thought leaders from numerous industries. More importantly, I spent countless hours reflecting on the gritty, real-world laterally violent incidents experienced by me and the conflict management experts at Vistelar, the company at which I now work and am a partner/owner.

I draw my experience from over 20 years of working in healthcare, law enforcement, and education as both a front-line worker and organizational leader. Additionally, I have worked with multiple organizations in helping them develop their own workplace violence prevention and intervention programming.

The experiences of the team at Vistelar date back more than 40 years and extend across the entire spectrum of human conflict, from the management of simple verbal disputes all the way through physical violence and the need for physical intervention. Vistelar helps organizations build safe and respectful workplaces via verbal and physical conflict management solutions. In my role at Vistelar, I work with such disciplines as healthcare, behavioral health, education, security, social services, home visitation, hospitality, customer service, transit, and law enforcement.

You can learn more about Vistelar in the section titled "Who is Vistelar" at the end of the book.

This book was developed as a resource for members of any community but the focus is on employees and leaders in workplaces.

By reading this book, you will gain the knowledge, skills, and abilities to:

- Reduce ambiguity in identifying lateral violence, workplace incivility, and toxic workplace tactics.

- Prevent lateral and workplace violence via the practice of "non-escalation."

- Recognize and mitigate gateway behaviors and other conditions that lead to workplace violence.

- Recognize pre-incident indicators that can be precursors to violence.

- Safely interact with people who are demonstrating laterally violent behaviors.

- Assist, fix, stop, and report professionally unacceptable behavior.

- Conduct a professional intervention or ethical override.

- De-escalate and recover from situations that could lead to violence.

- Act appropriately when faced with violence.

- Understand the need to report, document, and debrief workplace violence incidents.

- Create an environment that is emotionally and physically safer for everyone.

Additionally, if you are responsible for the development and implementation of an organization-wide workplace violence or psychosocial hazard prevention program, the information in this book will prove invaluable to you.

Again, the focus of this book is on lateral violence (non-physical, but harmful, behavior between members of a community) but, at times, the content will extend to the broader topic of workplace violence. For more in-depth information about workplace violence, I encourage you to contact us at Vistelar (please reference the section titled "Who is Vistelar" at the end of the book.

Jill Weisensel

PART ONE
Framing the Problem of Lateral Violence

....

CHAPTER ONE
Lateral Violence as Part of Workplace Violence

If I had only changed myself first ...

"When I was young and free and my imagination had no limits, I dreamed of changing the world. As I grew older and wiser and realized the world would not change I shortened my sights somewhat and decided to change only my country, but it too seemed immovable. As I grew into my twilight years I settled on changing only my family and those closest to me, but alas they would have none of it. Now as I lay on my deathbed and I suddenly realize that if I had only changed myself first, then by example I could perhaps have changed my family, and from their inspiration and encouragement to me I would have been better able to help my country and from there I may even have been able to change the world."

- From the tomb of an Anglican Bishop in Westminster Abbey, 1100 A.D.

The paradigm of acceptance of violence in the workplace must be abandoned. Instead, we must create environments of care by developing and reinforcing professional standards that are incompatible with emotional and physical violence.

We all know what acts of physical violence look like, but recognizing the subtle signs of lateral violence is much more difficult. However, it is critical in our efforts to eliminate workplace violence to understand the distinction, as lateral violence feeds directly into physical violence.

Lateral violence is any non-physical, but harmful, behavior between members of a community (e.g., workplace employees). This behavior can be passive-aggressive, aggressive, or even hostile.

The paradigm of acceptance of violence in the workplace must be abandoned. Instead, we must create environments of care by developing and reinforcing professional standards that are incompatible with emotional and physical violence.

While individual acts of lateral violence can appear relatively harmless, they ultimately create a toxic environment that takes a toll on employee morale and productivity, hindering the success of the organizations for which they work.

Historically, the term lateral violence has been used interchangeably with terms such as horizontal violence, bullying, incivility, hazing, disruptive behavior, relational aggression, and workplace dysfunction. These behaviors often slip under the radar as "innocent" remarks or actions that have ambiguous intent, but research has shown that these uncivil behaviors directly impact an employee's ability to effectively perform their job duties. (Cooper & Hoel, 2000)

The subtle nature and absence of a widely understood and agreed-upon definition of lateral violence contributes to the minimization and lack of recognition of its prevalence and subsequently makes it hard to identify, mitigate, regulate, enforce, and remove it from the workplace.

Although often associated with the nursing profession, the problem of lateral violence can exist in any environment. Anyone can engage in laterally violent behavior, but it is typically perpetrated by people who view themselves as superior to others. Organizational managers and more experienced employees are the most frequent perpetrators of lateral violence, making it difficult for lower-level or less experienced employees to report their abuse for fear of retaliation, among other reasons. This power dynamic can manifest itself in many subtle (and not so subtle) ways.

Even though lateral violence often slips under the radar, the blunt reality is that it can lead to physical violence and even death. For example, there is a direct correlation between workplace lateral violence and active shooter incidents. (Modell, 2013) Research has also indicated that behavior in response to lateral violence incidents includes professional disengagement, avoidance, intent to resign, and, most frighteningly, physical retaliation. (Morrison, Lindo, Aiken, & Chin, 2017) In another study referenced in the book *The Price of Incivility*, Drs. Christine Porath and Christine Pearson found that a shocking 94% of victims claim they settle their scores with the offenders, sometimes with physical violence

Therefore, lateral violence is not only an issue of improving workplace morale; it can be a matter of life and death.

It is important to note here that those who have been repeatedly bullied, disrespected, and treated with indignity, carry that frustration with them wherever they go. Their frustration can boil over and escalate to physical violence towards anyone at any time - not just towards fellow co-workers while at work.

Conversely, those consistently exposed to external stressors outside of work (e.g., relationship issues, divorce, child behavior, financial challenges, mental illness, and/or drug and alcohol addiction) can bring their frustration to work and unexpectedly lash out towards those within their organization.

The point being that lateral violence is not just a workplace problem. Lateral violence can lead to problems outside the workplace and, if present outside of work, can lead to problems within the workplace.

Laterally violent behaviors persist over time but often through discrete, relatively short-lived acts. They are often perpetrated by those with little to no connection to the abused. Instead, the only trigger may be random acts of bullying, including isolation, disrespect, and fear for their job and their future. We must not ever underestimate the "place we go" and the deeply painful emotions of fear, anger, hate, suffering, and contempt that we experience when we feel like we've been wronged. The core elements of underlying human emotion here can drive drastic behavioral responses.

> *"If you never heal from what hurt you, you'll bleed on those who didn't cut you."*
>
> - Author unknown

There is no single explanation for the prevalence of lateral violence in the workplace, but research has shown that institutional power structures, job-related stress, and organizational culture (including the behavioral expectations of the organization's underlying social contract) play a large role. (Englander & Raffalli, 2012) A social contract is an agreement of acceptable behavior amongst a group of people.

Workplace incivility is often described as "low intensity" conduct with ambiguous intent of harm. This includes being mildly (but regularly) rude or discourteous or violating behavioral norms in the workplace, such as the basic norm of mutual respect. It often manifests itself as the exchange of "seemingly inconsequential inconsiderate words and deeds that violate conventional norms of workplace conduct." (Porath & Pearson, 2013)

The description of "ambiguous intent of harm" is what distinguishes workplace incivility from other forms of interpersonal mistreatment. It is the vagueness of intent in these situations that make workplace incivility difficult to understand. Furthermore, whether or not behaviors or words are uncivil depends on how the receiver perceives them. Gossiping, exclusion, and hostility consistently rank among the top-cited forms of workplace incivility. (Bambi, Foà, De Felippis, Lucchini, Guazzini, & Rasero, 2018)

In the workplace, poorly managed lateral violence has serious implications, including compromised physical health, mental health, and other psychosocial hazards; high turnover; poor morale; low productivity; and reduced quality of products manufactured and services provided. Additionally, it directly leads to the loss of an organization's most valuable resource: employees. In one study, 60% of nurses who left their jobs within six months of hire attributed it to being bullied and harassed by veteran staff. In another, 80% of people reported holding back effort or lost time as a result of an uncivil interaction. (Porath & Pearson, 2012)

In essential services, such as healthcare, the cost of lateral violence is severe. In medicine, for instance, lateral violence negatively affects the quality of care, patient outcomes, and even mortality. Georgetown University's Dr. Christine Porath notes that workplace incivility can cause people to miss the transfer of critical information, resulting in a 17% loss in information retention, a 50% increase in medical mathematical errors, and a need for more time to make decisions. Facing consistent workplace incivility shuts down our brains at work, and in healthcare, it could be a matter of life and death.

Reduction in teamwork and functionality among first responders, corrections workers, and others engaged in high-risk work caused by lateral violence directly impacts their safety and the safety of others. These examples and more will be discussed in more detail later in the book.

Is Violence Really "Just Part of the Job?"

At one time or another, I'm sure we've all heard that dismissive phrase, that "so and so's" behavior is just the way it is and that there's "nothing you can do about it." But is that really true?

"To create an organizational culture incompatible with emotional and physical violence, we must first dispel the myth that toxic behaviors, disrespect, and violence are just 'part of the job.' Understanding this puts us on a path towards a safer and more respectful workplace experience."

- Joel Lashley, *Confidence in Conflict for Health Care Professionals: Creating an environment of care that is incompatible with violence*, Dispelling the Myth: Violence is Just Part of the Job, 2015, P.44

Just like with any other cycle of violence, if we accept this myth, we become paralyzed to act when action may be necessary.

Because so many people embrace this myth, the majority of schools are unsafe for children who find themselves endlessly bullied and hopeless.

Because of this myth, the majority of workplaces are unhealthy for adults who find themselves unable to navigate the personal politics, power struggles, and overall minefield of disrespectful and indignant behavior.

Because of this myth, residents and staff of group homes for people with psychiatric conditions and brain-based disorders are commonly locked in a daily cycle of violence and fear. And medical staff are assaulted on the job at rates at least seven times more than average.

Why is it that if a nurse threatened a patient, they would be fired without question? But when a co-worker makes an inappropriate comment, publicly berates, or threatens another employee, people are hesitant to take any action. It is because we have normalized these behaviors as acceptable, slowly, over time.

Just as we must ensure the safety of those under our care, we must ensure the emotional and physical safety of our employees—all employees.

Challenge yourself and others to avoid falling into the trap of the myth that violence is just part of the job. Avoid excuses for rudeness that include:

- *"That's just the way they talk. They didn't mean anything by it."*

- *"It's nothing. Ignore it."*

- *"We all face it. Toughen up."*

- *"I'd stay quiet if I were you. She is our star performer."*

- *"It's always been that way. No supervisor will do anything about it."*

All these excuses do is validate, perpetuate, and condone the behavior of those perpetrating!

The Role of Lateral Violence as Part of Workplace Violence

Incivility, bullying, and workplace violence are part of a larger complex phenomenon that includes a "constellation of harmful actions taken and those not taken" in the workplace. (Saltzberg, 2011, p. 229)

The phrase "actions taken and not taken" provides an overarching framework that includes perpetrating these acts, as well as failing to take action when action is warranted or required.

The U.S. Department of Labor defines workplace violence as "an action (verbal, written, or physical aggression) which is intended to control or cause, or is capable of causing, death or serious bodily injury to oneself or others, or property damage. Workplace violence includes abusive behavior toward authority, intimidating or harassing behavior, and threats."

OSHA addresses employee complaints of workplace violence and assesses employers based on OSHA's General Duty Clause, Section 5(a)(1) of the Occupational Safety and Health Act of 1970:

"(a) Each employer shall furnish to each employee employment and a place of employment which are free from recognized hazards that are causing or are likely to cause death or serious physical harm to employees."

Essentially, employers are on notice. They must provide a safe workplace environment, and allowing violent behaviors in any form is a failure to do so. Perhaps the failure to stop rumors or gossip is not as obvious as the need to post signage near a trip or fall hazard, but the underlying premise is the same: employers have a duty to identify workplace hazards and risks and take actions to mitigate them.

Additionally, employees will face adversity by being passed over for a raise, seeing others singlehandedly recognized for shared accomplishments or failing to achieve a long-sought-after promotion. Personal relationships and history between employees can also cause festering undercurrents and outright disagreements and, over time, can bubble to the surface in the form of resentment and retaliatory acts.

According to the Workplace Bullying Institute, the following acts and behaviors fall under the traditional definition of workplace bullying, which is a form of lateral violence:

> *Repeated, health-harming mistreatment of one or more persons (the targets) by one or more perpetrators that takes one or more of the following forms: verbal abuse; offensive conduct/behaviors (including nonverbal) which are threatening, humiliating, or intimidating; [and] work interference—sabotage—which prevents work from getting done.*

This includes:

- Making racial, ethnic, or religious jokes.
- Making jokes concerning another person's body shape, size, or physical ability/disability.
- Hazing.
- Intimidating.
- Coercion.
- Excluding coworkers.

- Making inappropriate comments (non-verbal or verbal).

- Making sexually provocative jokes or statements.

- Delivering unwanted sexual attention.

- Making jokes that violate what is socially acceptable.

- Playing intentionally hurtful practical jokes.

- Making other remarks that can be reasonably perceived as rude, offensive, or improper.

Any of these situations can lead to conflict, which can escalate to violence.

Bottom line, lateral violence (non-physical, but harmful, behavior between members of a community) can lead to physical violence and workplace violence from external sources which can manifest in these forms:

- Weapon use, such as with an armed physical assault.

- Unarmed physical assault, such as poking, slapping, or grabbing.

- Threats of harm or death (veiled, indirect, or direct).

- Stalking or displaying undue personal focus (in-person and/or on social media).

- Damaged property.

- Active shooter incidents.

- Sexual assault.

According to the U.S. Department of Labor, some two million American workers are victims of workplace violence each year; however, this number is likely much higher as workplace violence incidents often go unreported for a variety of reasons, such as fear of retaliation or the belief that it "just isn't worth it" to report it.

There is also greater visibility of the problem of workplace violence with the presence of security cameras and cell phone cameras. Almost every interaction is captured on video, which can show up instantly on social media or the evening news.

A 2018 survey by Everbridge/ASIS International found that 67% of executives and leaders were more concerned about employee safety than just two years prior. A 2019 survey by the Society for Human Resource Management found that incidents of violence were up 36% since 2012, and one out of seven employees feel unsafe at work.

Furthermore, the Workplace Violence Research Institute estimated costs of workplace violence to U.S. businesses at $360 billion per year due to turnover and decreased work productivity alone. Current hospital turnover is now at 19.5%, with a staggering 500,000 experienced nurses set to retire in 2022.

Core Causes of Lateral Violence

Institutional power structures (including rank, title, favoritism, and nepotism), job-related stress (distribution of an improper workload, for example), and organizational culture play large roles in enabling lateral violence. Internal politics (such as jockeying for promotions) and competing metrics (such as productivity or profit margin) also contribute.

The presence of lateral violence over time contributes to the acceptance and normalization of the behaviors as being both normal and appropriate, ultimately creating a new baseline of acceptable and expected behaviors.

The new behaviors become ingrained in the culture, and those who continue to behave that way view it as a rite of passage, or initiation, similar to hazing, i.e., *"Well, I was treated this way when I started, so now you're going to pay your dues too."*

When you're immersed in a workplace culture that has normalized lateral violence, it is nearly impossible to see and understand how toxic it truly is. It is often not until after an employee quits (or heads down a path resulting in termination) that they can look back, take a deep breath, and reflect on the situation. It is then and only then that they realize just how much the environment has been destroying them over time.

I have talked to dozens of people over the years who have quit their jobs. They often cite being exhausted, exasperated, and generally unsure of how it had come to that point. They talk about how miserable they were at work and how much better they feel—emotionally, mentally, and physically—just because they removed themselves from that environment. They cite leaving "bad bosses" and "toxic environments" far more than quitting because of the nature of the work itself.

The presence of lateral violence over time contributes to the acceptance and normalization of the behaviors as being both normal and appropriate, ultimately creating a new baseline of acceptable and expected behaviors.

It is heartbreaking to hear, but hindsight is always 20/20.

Laterally violent behaviors are often perpetuated by those who view themselves as superior to others (either explicitly by rank or title or implicitly through their unofficial role in the workplace or as a byproduct of their personal belief system). Please note that if there is an explicit hierarchical difference (such as legitimately being someone's boss, manager, or supervisor) between the offender and the victimized, this behavior is often categorized as "vertical violence."

Oftentimes, people believe or perceive that employees of lower rank or status are inferior to those of higher status. Examples of this power struggle play out daily in healthcare systems worldwide. Hospital administrators and patients often consider nurses inferior to physicians, certified nursing assistants inferior to nurses, and support staff inferior to all. Physicians often receive the praise, even though the nurse's skill and commitment directly improved patient outcomes. As a result, many nurses feel powerless and undervalued, leading to significant internal frustration. Some researchers believe that lateral violence is the outward expression of this frustration. (Bambi et al., 2018)

Someone's repeated unreasonable behavior, where the behavior creates a risk to health and safety, may be a result of power imbalances related to their position in the organization. A power difference may be caused by experience, age, the length of time the person has been with the organization, social position, or other factors between the person perpetrating the bullying behavior and the person or people who are targeted by the bullying behavior.

Additionally, increasing latent tensions, such as frustration related to the unequal power dynamic, can lead to overt conflicts and power struggles in the workplace. Overt conflict manifests itself as conflicts of interests, disputes of rights, visible signs of unequal power or treatment, and feelings of being unsupported with limited resources.

We have to move away from cultural expectations that teach and allow us to humiliate or dehumanize others as a way to achieve power or respect. We have to move away from cutthroat business environments that encourage and reward manipulative and harsh ways of getting the upper hand. We must challenge ourselves to transform the dynamic that it is acceptable for anyone to get away with treating others as inferior because of their social status.

> *We have to move away from cutthroat business environments that encourage and reward manipulative and harsh ways of getting the upper hand.*

Core Costs of Lateral Violence

As adults, we assume that we would have the freedom, resources, and autonomy to identify and walk away from an abusive and/or toxic situation. But with respect to workplace violence, we are obligated to return day in and day out to the scene (or source) of harassment (unless, of course, we quit).

The abuse that culminates in the professional world mirrors some of the long-term physiological and psychological effects of long-term victimization of school bullying.

If the benefit of retaining employees and preventing emotional trauma is not reason enough to end lateral violence, employers and organizational leadership should also consider the exceptional costs associated with condoning and maintaining a toxic workplace environment.

Consider these additional, non-insurable organizational costs and losses:

Production losses:

- Increased overhead costs while production is reduced.

- Time lost due to preoccupation with a negative situation.

- Reduced productivity as a result of workplace incivility. (Oyeleye, Hanson, O'Connor & Dunn, 2013)

- Production lost to absenteeism or presenteeism of the offender. Workplace incivility has been found to be a predictive factor of commitment to work (Smith et al., 2010) and absenteeism. (Bambi et al., 2018 and Zia ud-Din, 2017)

- Time lost due to internal transfers.

- Time lost when employees look for new jobs.

- Time lost to prepare a case in defense of a civil suit.

- Loss of skill or experience when a person leaves.

- Loss of invaluable institutional knowledge.

- Lower production rate of lesser experienced replacement

workers.

Wages lost:

- Interruption of work due to the negative situation.
- Cost of replacing staff (recruiting, onboarding).

According to the 2019 National Healthcare Retention & RN Staffing Report, published by Nursing Solutions, Inc., each percent change in nurse turnover will cost (or save) the average hospital an additional $328,400.

Associated costs:

- Investigations (internal and/or external).
- Implementing new reporting recommendations.
- Legal costs related to common law claims.
- Costs associated with training new employees.
- An increase in business insurance costs due to claims.

Intangible costs:

- Lower employee commitment resulting in lower performance, decreased motivation, decreased loyalty, decreased morale, and threat or damage to organizational reputation.

No organization will have insurance enough to cover the time and emotional toll of having an organizational culture and disposition of disrespecting others. For example, we often ignore (or fail to address) the substantial implications of allowing harmful statements, or "toxic talk," to go unchecked.

Generally speaking, it starts with "water cooler talk" or gossip during lunch breaks. What some perceive as harmless and spout off without a second thought may emotionally or professionally devastate others.

For example, consider a situation where a human resources employee had to make a tough executive decision, one that was not in favor of a friend of yours. Soon that friend is spreading rumors—unfactual, biased, or slanted information that led to the decision. Soon after, those rumors spiral and are injected with additional venom, anger, and frustration as they permeate throughout the organization. This slanted spiral of information leads to a dangerous polarization of events (or ideas) and often damages the reputations of all involved.

In addition to the steep individual emotional toil, defamation of character and injury to reputation lawsuits are costly and extremely time-consuming, taking years of dedicated legal resources to resolve.

Additional Consequences of Lateral Violence

Truly, the consequences and costs of lateral violence cannot be fully understood as standalone pieces; the sum is greater than its parts. The magnitude of organizational costs is compounded by the other, more elusive costs of workplace incivility, such as the specific costs to individuals. These costs extend to and have repercussions far beyond those who have been directly victimized. They extend to and are experienced by all employees immersed in a disrespectful and toxic culture.

Consider these staggering unethical costs to the individual, supported by decades of research, summarized in the groundbreaking meta-analysis study "Workplace incivility, lateral violence and bullying among nurses. A review about their prevalence and related factors," conducted by Bambi et al., 2018.

Psychosocial hazards and adverse health outcomes can include:

- Post-traumatic stress.

- Post-traumatic stress disorder.

- Depression.

- Anxiety. Workplace incivility has a positive predictive function to generate anxiety and burnout. (Bambi et al., 2018)

- Apathy.

- Loss of sleep.

- Loss of appetite.

- Lower self-esteem and/or self-confidence.

- Anger/rage.

- Chronic fatigue. Workplace incivility has a significant predictive factor for emotive exhaustion. (Spence-Laschinger HK, Leiter M, Day A, Gilin D, (2009)

- Compassion fatigue.

- Suicidal thoughts.

- Irritability.

- Nervousness of victimization and revictimization.

- Headaches, stomach aches, and/or abdominal pain.

- Nausea and stomach upset. Workplace incivility is directly correlated with physical symptoms. (Leiter MP, Price SL, Spence Laschinger HK, 2010)

- Social withdrawal.

- Obesity.

- Heart, lung, and/or liver disease.

- Cancer.

Negative impact on quality of life:

- Increased dread of going to work.

- Reduced job satisfaction. (Topa & Moriano, 2013)

- Burnout. There is a linear relationship between workplace incivility and burnout. (Elmblad R, Kodjebacheva G, Lebeck L, 2014)

- Increased propensity to leave/turnover intention.
  (Lieter et al., 2010)

- Increased chemical abuse
  (Vartia MA-L., 2013)

The slowly increasing awareness by employees that it is their right to have a safe and healthy workplace is exciting, but that's an example of something that should have happened a long time ago.

Employers need to realize that the "soft stuff" is really the "hard stuff," meaning that managing behaviors in the workplace can affect the bottom line much more than sales analytics and penny-pinching.

Employers need to realize that the "soft stuff" is really the "hard stuff," meaning that managing behaviors in the workplace can affect the bottom line much more than sales analytics and penny-pinching.

Key Takeaways

- We must abandon the acceptance of violence and incivility in the workplace.
- Lateral violence is non-physical, but harmful, behavior between members of a community (e.g., workplace employees).
- Institutional power structures, job-related stress, and organizational culture play a large role in enabling workplace violence. Internal politics and competition also contribute.
- We can combat the myth that violence is "just part of the job" by developing and reinforcing professional standards that are incompatible with emotional and physical violence.
- The true costs of lateral violence, incivility, and working in a toxic workplace culture are measurable by the effects on both the organization and the individual.
- Feeling disrespected and undervalued in the workplace is the number one reason people quit their jobs.

CHAPTER TWO

Understanding Lateral Violence on a Deeper Level

No one wants to recognize (or admit) that they are a victim (of anything), so we often fail to identify certain behaviors as victimizing. But no matter how we personally understand and define lateral violence, bullying, abuse, discrimination, or harassment, it is time to expand our understanding of unacceptable behaviors. Regardless if the person engaging in unacceptable behavior is a co-worker, manager, outside client, or member of the public, it is also time to recognize the behaviors that we have become desensitized to as a result of constant exposure to them.

Let's take a look at this short example:

Once while I was waiting to meet with a physician and his staff about a patient who had threatened his life, I struck up a conversation with one of his nurses. I asked her if anything like this had ever happened before. She said it hadn't and that she was in shock over the whole incident. Nonetheless, she thought the whole thing was silly and that the doctor was making way too many things.

I then asked her how long she'd been in nursing. She explained she'd been a nurse for more than 30 years and worked in many specialties as an RN and Master Degree prepared nurse. I then asked her if she'd experienced much violence on the job. She replied, 'Not really. Things really aren't that bad. A little conflict here and there is just part of the job.' I then asked her if a patient or visitor had ever shoved her, and she said, 'Sure.' I then asked her if anyone had ever slapped her, and she said, 'I've been slapped a couple of times, sure.' I asked her if she'd ever been kicked, punched, grabbed, or spit on, and she answered yes to all. Finally, I asked her what sort of behavior she considered violent. She replied, 'Yeah, I see where you're going, but I used to be an E.R. nurse. A lot of that stuff happened there. After that, I would only get attacked by someone once in a blue moon.'

- Joel Lashley, *Confidence in Conflict for Health Care Professionals: Creating an environment of care that is incompatible with violence*, Dispelling the Myth: Things Really Aren't that Bad, 2015, P46

If you work as a nurse in a hospital, you are at least five times more likely to be physically assaulted than the average wage-earner, and if you work in an emergency department, that number at least doubles. It's time to ask ourselves if this is really the way it has to be. Are we getting anywhere by denying there's a problem or becoming desensitized to what is going on around us? Are we getting any safer? Have our false notions of acceptable behavior in our workplace environments perpetuated a myth and a standard that keeps us locked in a cycle of violence?

So, what is the solution? Perhaps one can be found by raising our expectations of acceptable behavior, instilling a sense of social responsibility and a shared professional standard of organizational civility. In order to do this, we must expand our understanding of violence and the various behaviors and dynamics that accompany it, in addition to providing the training needed to manage it.

Expanding Our Understanding of Violence: Identifying and Understanding the Cycle of Violence

By expanding our definition of violence and refusing to accept violence as the norm, we will be better equipped to:

1. Identify lateral violence.
2. Recognize the dynamics that may either intentionally or inadvertently contribute to an environment that condones violence.
3. Assess the observable behaviors that signal the potential for violent assaults.

When people curse and otherwise behave inappropriately, they are sending out, in a sense, verbal "radar waves" to see what signals bounce back. When the answer they receive is silence, they begin to gain power and authority over the group.

Once they become comfortable making others uncomfortable, they begin to turn up the heat. Often this takes the form of yelling or shouting. When we remain silent, they also become comfortable shouting at us. Then they begin to threaten us, often in the form of an implied or veiled threat. Examples are, "*Make me look bad in a meeting again and see what happens*" or "*If she calls in sick on a weekend again she'll be sorry.*"

Once people become comfortable implying they will hurt us, they often escalate by blatantly threatening us by saying direct things like, "*If you take credit for my work again I will slash your car tires!*"

In healthcare, perhaps more than in any other profession, co-workers, patients, and family members routinely threaten staff with absolute impunity and it has become the norm. So, when people get comfortable threatening us and can do so with impunity, why not hit us? That is the question we often place in the minds of our attackers when we fail to train to manage aggression and set limits on bad behavior.

All cycles of interpersonal violence develop this way, whether between nations or individuals, whether it's a schoolyard fight or a long-term domestic violence relationship. In our personal lives and in the workplace, gateway behaviors, the dynamics of power and control, and language are all components in the cycle of violence.

Identifying Toxic Tactics and Gateway Behaviors

Gateway behaviors are defined as actions that can be a precursor to violence, such as:

- Shouting.
- Cursing.
- Name-calling.
- Insulting.
- Displays of prejudice.
- Dignity violations.
- Intimidating postures.
- Aggressive positioning.
- Indirect threats.

Gateway Behaviors to Violence:

When gateway behaviors are observed, trained professionals can reliably minimize anxiety, assuage fear, set limits on inappropriate behaviors, and address underlying issues, thereby diffusing the potential for violence. That formula leads to safer environments and better results.

If we intervene early in the gateway behavior cycle, we can stop the journey toward violence. If we can stop people from cursing and yelling, they may not graduate to threatening and violent behavior. Ultimately, it is much easier to stop someone from yelling than it is to stop them from hitting. But we can't even begin if we don't understand how or when.

The person with the worst behavior sets the tone for what is acceptable for everyone else. Nothing will make exemplary employees leave faster than watching a leader tolerate an inexcusable employee.

When witnessing laterally violent behavior, people often:

- Deny it.

- Distract themselves from it, so it looks like they don't know it's going on.

- Remove themselves from the situation.

- Laugh to convince themselves it isn't serious.

- Overtly ignore it, hoping it goes away.

- Join in, hoping the perpetrator doesn't target them, too.

Here's the point: If a manager says nothing when they overhear sexual harassment, they have condoned it and become an enabler of it. Saying nothing tacitly empowers the actor to continue the behavior by sending the message you are unconcerned by it. Inappropriate behavior that goes uncorrected (or inconsistently addressed) becomes the acceptable norm.

"Tolerance for the little things makes the bigger things more likely."
– Joel Lashley, Author and Conflict Management Expert

Everyone knows not to drop f-bombs in church or talk loudly in a library. But why do so many people yell, curse, and threaten in a hospital? Is it simply because some people behave badly when they're sick? Or is it because they believe they are entitled to behave badly because they're sick? Perhaps it's because healthcare workers believe employees and patients have a right to behave badly. In reality, it's all of the above.

Once we decide to set limits on bad behaviors, we'll all be safer. But if we set the bar too low, we often end up acting too late. For example, in healthcare, we have to remind ourselves that nice people don't hurt us—angry, anti-social, and threatening people do! Because behaviors are connected, people usually build up to violence. They start with refusing to follow visiting hours, refusing to wear visitors' passes, cursing, yelling, or threatening well before they attack. If we start to set limits when people first begin to violate our social contract, they are more likely to become cooperative and less likely to become violent.

Abusive Workplace Behavior and the Dynamics of Power and Control

Workplace bullying, which is a form of lateral violence, is defined as "systematic aggressive communication, manipulation of work, and acts aimed at humiliating or degrading one or more individuals that create an unhealthy and unprofessional power imbalance between bully and target(s), results in psychological consequences for targets and co-workers, and cost enormous monetary damage to an organization's bottom line." (Mattice, C.M., & Garman, K, 2010)

"The difference between how a person treats the powerless versus the powerful is as good a measure of human character as I know."

- Dr. Robert Sutton, Stanford Professor and author of *Good Boss, Bad Boss*

Remember, people talk differently (using a harsher tone or more insulting word choice) and use different tactics when they believe others have an obligation to them and/or are inferior to them. This often manifests itself as disrespectful and indignant behavior.

A comprehensive review of the literature related to abusive workplace practices (refer to the Reference and Resource section of this book) results in the identification of numerous laterally violent behaviors. Most behaviors fall into the categories of discrimination, harassment, bullying, and retaliation. The below list includes those categories and their associated tactics; however, please note that certain behaviors may fall into more than one category, depending on the specific context.

Displaying discrimination:

- Denying access to information, supervision, consultation, or resources such that it has a detriment to the target.

- Excluding (generally targeted exclusion) someone from workplace activities (social or physical isolation).

- Withholding information that is vital for effective work performance.

- Setting unreasonable timelines or constantly changing deadlines.

- Setting tasks that are unreasonably below or beyond the target's skill level.

- Leveraging harsh criticism or having a different work standard for the target of abuse.

- Manipulating job content by limiting the variety or use of skills; replacing key projects with trivial tasks.

- Using the silent treatment or exclusion.
- Subjecting the target to excessive scrutiny at work (e.g., surveillance, micro-management, monitoring).

Displaying harassment:

- Micromanagement of tasks.
- Making up rules on the fly (without rules or policy to support).
- Encouraging people to turn against someone.
- Changing work arrangements (e.g., rosters or leave) to inconvenience the target.
- Staring with the intent to intimidate.

Bullying:

- Abusive, insulting, or offensive language or comments; disrespect and devaluing.
- Starting or failing to stop destructive rumors or gossip.
- Launching a campaign to oust someone, and the effort is not stopped by the employer.
- Unjustly discounting an employee's thoughts or feelings; overtly ignoring opinions or views.
- Yelling, screaming, or throwing a tantrum to publicly embarrass an employee.
- Disregarding exemplary work.
- Abusing the performance review process by lying about the target's performance.
- Stealing credit for someone else's work.
- Spreading negative rumors or false information about the target.

- Setting an unreasonable workload schedule or pace.

- Creating unrealistic demands (deadlines and duties).

- Failing to provide a physically safe environment.

- Withholding necessary equipment from the target.

- The employer encourages the target to quit rather than face further mistreatment.

Retaliation:

- Assigning an undesirable work assignment or sabotaging tasks related to an assignment.

- Acting in a way that impedes the target's career development; preventing access to opportunities for growth.

- Declaring the target as insubordinate for failing to follow arbitrary requests or commands.

- Leveraging unjustified criticism or complaints; false accusal.

- Publicly disclosing private or confidential information to humiliate an employee.

Even if your organization has the current luxury of a healthy culture, please do not dismiss or overlook the fact that even the healthiest organizational cultures can still have "pockets of toxicity" within them. This can result from varied working conditions found in different departments but are more often the result of varied (micro cultural) perceptions from different identity groups towards particular leaders. (Sull & Sull, 2022)

Understanding the Role of Language and Mitigated Speech

Mitigated speech was popularized by Malcolm Gladwell in his book, *Outliers*, where he defines mitigated speech as "any attempt to downplay or sugarcoat the meaning of what is being said," especially to those in authority (or in perceived positions of authority). In some cases, mitigation can be a good thing. Mitigating your speech may be the most polite and respectful way to get your point across. In others, if you mitigate too much, you may not get your point across to the intended party at all.

It is important to understand the role of mitigated speech in identifying laterally violent behaviors and comments and in how they are reported—or not. Dysfunctional communication structures and the use of mitigated speech directly hinder the ability of employees to report incidents or advocate for themselves in the moment.

For example, someone's position, title, rank, and relationship will directly impact how a message is conveyed. For example, if the co-pilot of a plane was concerned about the course coordinates set by the primary pilot, the co-pilot may not necessarily be direct in correcting the pilot's error because their role/position is seen as secondary, or inferior to, the pilot. However, if the co-pilot fails to call out the error or make the correction, it could have devastating results.

The co-pilot must now find a way to balance the need to communicate against the imbalanced power structure of their relationship and roles by communicating the concern as a hint, or suggestion, rather than as a command. These are described as varying degrees of mitigation with which we make suggestions to authority.

Let's take a look at what mitigated speech sounds like and how it plays out in a real-life example. Using the six degrees of mitigation, let's try to make the point that you'd like a coworker to stop using sexist language:

1. The first option is to use a command:

    "Don't talk about women like that."

    This is the most direct way of communicating a point that you want to make. It's zero mitigation. It may not come across as sensitive, but it is true. However, using a command is also likely to be the most confrontational in the moment.

2. The second option is to use a team obligation statement:
   "We shouldn't talk about women like that."

   The use of the word "we" is less direct and is "softer" communication. By using the word "we," you position yourself as an ally, or an advocate, while also expressing disapproval.

3. The third option is to give a suggestion:
   "I don't think we should talk about women that way."

   Implicit in this statement is "we're in this together" and "I think it is a good idea to stop." It also gives the speaker an opportunity to save face and agree with you.

4. The fourth option is to offer a query:
   "How would you feel if someone talked about your sister like that?"

   This is a "softer suggestion" because the speaker is conceding that they are not in charge and it offers perspective taking (or, technically, perspective giving) in the moment. It allows the speaker to rethink the repercussions of what was just said.

5. The fifth option is to state a preference:
   "I'd like it if you'd stop making comments like that."

   This states a personal preference but is more direct. Explicit in this statement is the expectation of what you'd like the speaker to do in the future.

6. The sixth option, and the most mitigated way to make a point, is to offer a hint:
   "That statement is a little harsh."

   A "hint" is the most mitigated a statement can be and the least likely to get the result you're looking for because it is the most difficult to decode and the easiest to refuse. However, if you modify the engagement phrase and combine it with a query:

   "That statement is a little harsh, don't you think?"

You may be able to bridge the moment into a productive conversation about why you felt the statement was harsh (because it was demeaning to women).

Furthermore, people who communicate with lots of hints often don't communicate clearly to people who communicate more directly. And the problem compounds if (a) those who prefer mitigated speech are intimidated by those who use direct speech and/or (b) those who prefer mitigated speech really want those who use direct speech to like them and thus try not to say anything that might cause relational tension.

To that end, those who prefer mitigated speech often use a "hedge," a mitigating word, sound, or construction used to lessen the impact of an utterance due to constraints on the interaction between the speaker and addressee. When used positively, hedges are used to "soften the blow," avoid the appearance of bragging, and improve politeness (generally understood as "having tact" or being tactful). If used negatively, a hedge could result in the delivery of a passive-aggressive statement whereas you may think you're being polite, but others think you're being a jerk. It could be the difference between "what was said," and "what was meant by what was said."

Hedges are typically adjectives, adverbs, or clauses and may be intentionally or unintentionally employed in both written and spoken communication. Consider this example. Would you rather your boss say to you:

"There are things we need to address,"

- or -

"There are just a few small things we need to address."

By adding the word "few" and the adjective "small," the speaker relays a more precise message (it is far less vague and open-ended) and also softens the blow to the receiver.

The above sentence could be further improved by changing the word "address." The word "address" could mean any number of things to different people, and quite frankly, if on Friday my boss said, *"There are things we need to address on Monday,"* and then told me nothing further, I would be a complete wreck all weekend. My mind would spin out on all of the things I possibly could have done recently that we need to "address."

We could restructure this sentence in numerous ways and modify the delivery of the words to flush out dozens of possible reactions by the receiver. For the sake of this example, if you know that your employee will overthink and worry about what is coming on Monday, you need to be more direct in your message.

However, direct does not mean harsh. It is possible to be "firm but polite." You can deliver a strong message with a soft tone. In the above example, we could deliver a more precise message by stating:

"On Monday, I'd like to talk with you about that quarterly report. There are a few parts we can clean up."

And even if you don't know how the employee will react, it is more respectful and more likely to elicit your intended result by being impeccable with your words. Always say what you mean and mean what you say—the precision of word choice matters. Words mean different things to different people as a result of varying cultural backgrounds, experiences, biases, and assumptions, and it is important to be mindful of that when interacting with someone.

With the goal of what to say and when to say it in mind, researchers Megan Reitz and John Higgins have identified multiple intertwined issues in their book *Speak Up: Say What Needs to be Said and Hear What Needs to be Heard.* Reitz and Higgins state that multiple factors come into play when making a decision to speak up or listen up at work. First, people must trust in the value of their (or the other person's) opinion and weigh that against the risk of speaking up (or being spoken up to). Secondly, all parties involved must navigate an ever-changing political environment, assessing how various social titles and labels (such as gender, age, job title, and race) affect speaking up and listening up while also having the "capacity to judge how to say things" or "invite things to be said in the moment."

All of those factors directly impact what is said, how it is said, when it is said, and who says it. This is a far too overlooked and undervalued construct playing out in the workplace, especially as it relates to workplace incivility in understanding who has a voice and the nature and quality of feedback offered to those in leadership roles.

In terms of soliciting valuable feedback, your approachability matters. What you say, why you say it, and how you say it matters in the eyes of those you are working with.

In terms of soliciting valuable feedback, your approachability matters. What you say, why you say it, and how you say it matters in the eyes of those you are working with. If you think you are coming across as genuine and sincere, but your body language and tone send the message that you don't care, that is the message that will be received by others. People hear what they see and only remember how you made them feel.

Trauma in the Workplace

Trauma is the exposure to an incident or series of events that is emotionally or physically harmful or life-threatening, or that has lasting adverse effects on an individual's well-being. For the purpose of this book, the causes of trauma include physical, sexual, situational, contextual, cultural, and emotional abuse, such as the emotional abuse someone is subjected to as the target of laterally violent behaviors over time.

"Trauma not transformed will be trauma transferred."
– Ashley Judd, American actress

Trauma comes in many forms, including vicarious, which results from exposure to hearing (or being witness to) the trauma of others. This is often seen in military personnel, law enforcement/first responders, counselors, and healthcare workers, as they are typically exposed to a higher number of traumatic incidents over the course of their careers than those not working in those professions.

The potential health implications of traumatic events do not have to be lifelong. We can create environments and cultural/social systems that employ trauma-informed principles. This includes creating a supportive atmosphere (rather than a defensive one) and a caring, inclusive environment for everyone. A supportive atmosphere is made possible by creating a functional communication structure supported by policies, consistent training, and follow-through.

First, we must acknowledge that everyone's life experiences are different and recognize how organizational practices may trigger painful memories and re-traumatize those with trauma histories. Organizations may inadvertently create stressful or toxic environments that interfere with the well-being of staff and the organizational mission.

This acknowledgment can also be framed as being *trauma responsive.* Being trauma responsive (or having trauma responsiveness), means acknowledging the existence of past trauma (in both ourselves and in others) potentially impacting current behaviors. The key point to remember is that everyone has had past events and experiences that may prevent them from responding or performing now, in the moment, as you may expect them to. Trauma responsiveness is an effective approach to minimize the chance of re-traumatizing someone.

Trauma responsiveness allows us to create an environment that provides:

- Safety: Where all people have the right to be physically and psychologically safe.

- Trustworthiness and transparency: Where operations are conducted with transparency to build and maintain trust.

- Peer support: Where interpersonal relationships contribute to establishing hope, trust, and collaboration.

- Collaboration and mutuality: Where power differences are leveled between organizational staff, demonstrating that healing happens in relationships and the sharing of power and decision making.

- Empowerment: Where employees are provided a voice and a choice, building on individuals' strengths, experiences, and resiliency.

- Common ground: Where cultural stereotypes and biases are cast aside, and policies and practices that are responsive to racial, ethnic, and cultural needs are incorporated.

"An environment that is not safe to disagree is not an environment focused on growth - it's an environment focused on control."

– Wendi Jade, American author

Why Don't People Report?

The subtlety of behaviors, such as not including someone in an email list or failing to give someone the time needed to prepare for a meeting, is often viewed as trivial. But when you evaluate those behaviors in the broader context of the environment described above, we begin to see just how pervasive and destructive they are.

Despite best efforts to research prevalence, laterally violent behaviors often go unreported for a variety of reasons, including the primary driver of strong emotions such as fear and embarrassment:

- Many studies have shown that the majority of employees are too scared to report for fear of being seen as untrustworthy or a troublemaker.

- People are also afraid of the threat to their personal standing, professional status, being singled out or isolated, and being overworked. Fear is understood as inhibiting all reporting.

- Many employees fear coming forward because they don't have the confidence in the leader to do what is right.

- Employees fear accusations of incompetence, or they think their employer might assume they were the cause of the violence.

- Employees may be embarrassed and hesitant to report violent behavior.

- Employees may feel embarrassment or fear of shame or the response of management or friends.

Some of the additional reasons why people don't report include:

- The lack of a consistent definition of violence or the bar being set too high to be considered violence.

- A pervasive acceptance of threatening behavior and violence as part of the job.

- A belief that a threat of violence is not significant enough to report.

- Not knowing what to do. Employees may not know what constitutes inappropriate behavior or may be unaware of internal reporting systems.

- Lack of supervisor support.

- The role of the person using the behaviors: is the person a high performer? A friend of the boss? The boss?

- Someone in a supervisory role is the offender.

You can work to mitigate employees' fears about reporting by:

- Raising awareness of lateral violence.

- Educating about the importance of reporting and the damaging personal and organization costs associated with not reporting.

- Being open and transparent about not tolerating laterally violent behaviors and the need to create a safe and inclusive environment for everyone.

- Consistently responding to and following up to reported incidents.

Key Takeaways

- Tolerance for the little things makes the big things more likely. We must raise our expectations of professionally acceptable behavior.
- Gateway behaviors, the dynamics of power and control, and language are all components in the cycle of violence.
- If we intervene early in the gateway behavior cycle, we can stop the journey toward violence.
- As we get older, bullying doesn't disappear. The methods and tactics just become more subtle and ambiguous.
- Understand the role of mitigated speech and leverage the power of the various degrees of mitigation when addressing issues in the workplace.
- Trauma responsiveness refers to the way caring people are trained to respond to the emotional injuries and scars of trauma and reduces the chance that we will re-traumatize someone.
- Workplace violence incidents often go unreported for reasons such as not knowing what behaviors to report, fear of retaliation, and embarrassment in facing co-workers.

CHAPTER THREE

Creating an Environment that is Incompatible with Emotional and Physical Violence

"Act as if what you do makes a difference. It does."

– William James, philosopher and father of American psychology

In an analysis of 1.4 million Glassdoor reviews about company culture from people who have left their jobs, researchers Charlie and Donald Sull found what they call the "Toxic 5," the top themes that create a toxic corporate culture:

1. Lack of inclusion. Being non-inclusive or condoning an environment where people feel as if they are not being treated fairly because of their identity.

2. Disrespect. Being disrespected or feeling as if they are not respected.

3. Unethical behavior. Engaging in unethical behavior, such as dishonesty, lack of integrity, or failing to act within policy.

4. Cutthroat behavior. Engaging in cutthroat behavior, or people actively going out of their way to undermine or sabotage others.

5. Abusive Managers. Having abusive managers, those who overly criticize, discriminate, micromanage, and gaslight.

These five themes are above and beyond the more minute things people "grumble" or complain about at work. They are collectively, by far, the largest predictors of destroying quality of life and driving talented people out the door.

So then, to create a healthy workplace culture, we must first work to ensure we are not participating in or perpetuating any of those behaviors, or any of the behaviors mentioned in previous chapters.. Then secondly, we must work to build a collective environment that will not allow these behaviors to exist. We must build a value-based culture based on respect, integrity, diversity, and collaboration.

We all have a role to play in protecting, maintaining, and restoring dignity to and for all.

Creating an environment that is incompatible with emotional and physical violence will take a completely mobilized community, one that embraces a shared sense of social responsibility and is motivated by a new core philosophy: *treating all people with dignity by showing respect.*

We all have a role to play in protecting, maintaining, and restoring dignity to and for all.

Culture drives behavior, and behavior drives outcomes. Habits, good or bad, do not just exist at the individual level. When replicated across a group, habits create culture. By creating a shared culture of civility, you will drastically improve your team's willingness to help, creativity, and resource sharing.

If we are working to build a safer and more respectful community culture, the first question we must ask ourselves is, "Whose behavior are we trying to change?"

The answer is: Ours. Us. All of us. We all have a role to play.

It isn't just about your business, your individual title, or your specific role. Eradicating laterally violent behaviors is about the entire process. And that process of developing and maintaining your social contract, your core philosophy, your culture, and your brand includes your entire organizational community. For each member, it has to be about being a part of something greater than themselves, finding a way to contribute, and finding a way to champion the common good.

At every juncture of that process, that journey—whether it involves a customer, client, or employee—we must work to meet, exceed, and reinforce that culture.

Every interaction with someone is understood as an opportunity to build or destroy trust, and every piece of service delivery matters to the overall experience and performance within the organization. There are multiple moments and multiple touchpoints throughout the journey that will involve every individual that interfaces with them, including all of the contributions from the employees that you don't "see," the back-of-the-house-type staff who provide crucial services.

So here, to reinforce this point, just like security and safety are everybody's business, so is the way in which you and your co-workers interface with the public on a daily basis. For example, when people come to your organization with a question, they look for people who look like they work there to answer it; they don't care whether your employee works in customer service or not.

They don't care about their title. Or their specific role. All they care about is getting an answer to their question or getting a resolution to their problem. And to that end ... Everyone has a role to play in that service delivery, in living up to your promise, to your brand, and to your organizational reputation.

People will remember any part of the journey where that promise was not met. From the moment they walk in and judge how the place looks, to the first person they see and interact with, to the janitorial staff and the lunchroom staff, to the administrative staff, faculty, specialized staff, and all of those employees, including and up to the leadership in the C-suite. Everyone has to live up to that promise, brand, and culture. Living up to that promise is everybody's business.

The bottom line is that we all have to be part of the solution, or we very well could be part of the problem. Remember:

- What you permit, you promote.

- Doing nothing is never a neutral option.

- Nothing changes if nothing changes.

"This is a story about four people named Everybody, Somebody, Anybody, and Nobody. There was an important job to be done and Everybody was sure that Somebody would do it. Anybody could have done it, but Nobody did it. Somebody got angry about that, because it was Everybody's job. Everybody thought Anybody could do it, but Nobody realized that Everybody wouldn't do it. It ended up that Everybody blamed Somebody when Nobody did what Anyone could have."

– Author unknown

Building a Culture of Shared Social Responsibility

The following section outlines action steps you can take to build a culture of shared social responsibility. The steps include:

1. Mobilizing the strong opinion leaders.
2. Assessing community readiness.
3. Building a primary prevention and behavior change platform.
4. Creating a new social contract.

Step One: Mobilizing the Strong Opinion Leaders

The first step in creating a culture of shared social responsibility is to mobilize the strong opinion leaders, the role models, and leaders (both formal and informal) within your organization.

Think about it: How many times have you walked into a store or school and noticed the "hate-free zone" or "bully-free zone" sign on a wall? Yet, there are still plenty of hateful and harmful actions taking place and disrespectful comments being made in the space.

While there's a time and place for signage, awareness-raising alone does not lead to behavior change. The "hate-free zone" sign on the wall doesn't stop the behaviors from happening. It is the ethical presence of those in the room that stops those behaviors from happening.

> *"Bullying cannot systemically exist within an organization or group without the consent, cooperation, and participation of the leadership."*
>
> – Joel Lashley

Strong opinion leaders educate their circle of influence, and that circle will educate theirs, and so on. For a complete cultural shift to take hold, it has to be completely understood, accepted, and implemented through a top-down approach. It has to be addressed at all levels of the organization, and leaders must draw a hard line in the sand and become intolerant of any behaviors falling below that line. The goal is to stop all behaviors that are harming others. Period.

This may truly be the most critical point of this book: To raise expectations and implement true organizational change, you need strong leadership. But what does strong leadership look like?

Ethical Presence and Credibility of Character

Strong leaders—those who can be trusted, believed, respected, and heard—are both ethical and credible. They must have a highly professional bearing that drives standards of excellence. It is that bearing—that person's presence—that raises the standards and expectations for all the people in the room and everyone in the organization.

Always be responsible for the energy you bring into a space.

As a leader who trains other leaders, I remind you that "lead" is a verb and leadership actions must be intentional. The first form of leadership is self-leadership. Your goal is not to create followers; it is to create more leaders. I implore you to reflect on the following questions as they relate to the need for ethical presence and credibility of character:

1. Are you setting your best foot forward and consistently representing the most professional version of yourself?
2. When you walk into a room, does it get better or worse? Does it get emotionally and physically safer for everyone there, or not?
3. When you walk into a room, are people happy you are there? Do they change their behavior (for better or worse) because of your presence?
4. Are they safer because you are there?

"Leadership is about making others better as a result of your presence and making sure that impact lasts in your absence."

– Sheryl Sandberg, past Chief Operating Officer at Facebook

A Note About the Importance of Creating a Supportive Atmosphere

Employees will not be able to talk through anything effectively if they feel threatened in any way and/or enter a defensive state of being. The company at which I work, Vistelar, trains how to maintain your emotional equilibrium, even in the face of physical and mental stressors.

Physical stressors can range from:

- Environmental conditions such as hot/cold/wet, noisy, bright, or strong odors.
- Physiological conditions such as sleep deprivation, dehydration, and malnutrition.

And mental stressors range from:

- Cognitive stressors such as too much or too little sensory overload, isolation, uncertainty, unpredictability, and varying organizational dynamics.

- Emotional stressors such as fear, anxiety-producing threats, grief, resentment, boredom, frustration, and conflicting motives.

It is critical when having courageous, crucial, or critical conversations with people that you take into account their state of being. Are they calm, relaxed, and balanced? Or are they stressed, uncomfortable and imbalanced? You must do everything possible to ensure they remain in a calm, balanced state of being, or they literally—physiologically and emotionally speaking—will not be able to communicate effectively. Plainly put, when a person feels unsafe, they become defensive. And when they feel disrespected, they can easily go on the offensive.

Here's why:

When we feel threatened, regardless of the stressor, our body's fight or flight stress response kicks in, triggering an entire cascade of emotional, physiological, and psychological effects. Presenting all of these effects is beyond the scope of this book, but it is important to note that when the fight or flight response kicks in:

- Our heart rate goes up and our ability to think logically goes down.

- Our breathing rate and blood pressure increase while our fine concentration decreases.

- Our openness to new ideas is reduced and our thinking becomes muddled.

- Our interpersonal communication becomes defensive.

Even if you "do everything right," the person you are speaking with may become defensive. However, it is imperative that you maintain communication alignment and convey a message of respect and sincerity throughout your interaction to give you (and them) the best chance of a successful and professionally positive outcome. To maintain communication alignment, all of your proxemics (distance), non-verbals (expressions and other body language), verbals (word choices), and para-verbals (tone and volume of voice) must match your intended message. If you intend to show empathy, but your facial expression shows irritation, it won't matter how sincerely you try to deliver your words.

For more information on any of these concepts, please reference the section titled "Who is Vistelar" at the end of the book.

Modeling Behaviors and Behavioral Regulation

As Eleanor Roosevelt once said, *"It is not fair to ask of others what you are unwilling to do yourself."* Fellow employees will only do what you ask them to do when they believe in you.

Modeling behavior is key.

When a leader models the right behavior, is explicit in their expectations for behavior and consistently follows through in the management of behaviors, they help you construct a new social contract - a new set of agreed-upon and acceptable behaviors. This social contract will create an environment incompatible with emotional and physical violence; you will have created and consistently reinforced an environment that won't allow it.

"As much as I believe in tolerance and fairness, I have never lost a wink of sleep about being unapologetically intolerant of anyone who refuses to show respect for those around them."

– Dr. Robert Sutton

In calibrating new baseline behaviors—those behaviors that are going to be understood as "normal" or "acceptable" in your organization—the need for a supervisor to "write someone up" or issue a written letter comes far after the failure of other ways to regulate group behavioral expectations. Behavioral regulation—over punitive management—is the most desirable way to achieve and sustain a cultural shift.

Behavior regulation comes in three forms:

1. Self-motivation and self-regulation. This behavior should be easy to see; it is represented by your high achievers. Those who do the right thing, at the right time, for the right reasons, and in the right way, simply because it's the right thing to do. It is who they are. These people often become "unofficial" leaders in your organization—influencers—who have no prescribed authority through rank or title alone.

2. Peer regulation. This happens when the group's behavior influences those of others. It is the desire to be accepted by the group that often changes and normalizes the behaviors of others. If someone acts in a way that is determined unacceptable by the group, the group simply tells them to "knock it off" or offers a "tap out." This group does not necessarily represent the majority of employees; they could just be a highly influential group of people (representing an "in-group" that the new employee wishes to be a part of).

3. The need for a supervisor to address inappropriate behaviors. This could be as simple as a short conversation identifying the behavior(s) in question and then re-stating how those behaviors do not match the values and expectations of the organization. This can and should be handled tactfully and respectfully, with no formal repercussions.

Only if all of these forms of regulation have failed to address the inappropriate behaviors should the need arise to act upon formal disciplinary measures. Too often, young supervisors (and even experienced leaders) fail to see this and fail to understand, work through, develop, and support the power and influence of the other levels.

Setting and Enforcing Expectations

The failure to explicitly state clearly defined expectations sets employees (especially new ones) up for failure. And the failure to identify the need for and have crucial conversations as soon as you witness the behavior often leads to the need for harsher forms of reprimand farther down the road and often leads to additional and unnecessary frustration for all employees involved.

"In general, when we are unsure of ourselves, when the institution is unclear or ambiguous, we are most likely to look to and accept the actions of others as correct."

– Robert Cialdini, psychologist, author, and speaker

Yes, oftentimes, those conversations can be difficult and awkward to have, but the costs of feeling awkward in the moment are far less than the loss of an exemplary employee because you allowed them to stray too far off the path of your expectations or organizational standards.

We can all probably think of at least one employee we've worked with whom this has happened to. They were once highly motivated with a great attitude. They were fun to work with, highly efficient, and effective. Then someday, "out of nowhere," something changed. Something happened, and that employee was no longer fun to work with, and then they were far from exemplary.

Usually, this leads to supervisors labeling that employee as having a bad attitude or being lazy, and they never stop to ask themselves what happened. What happened to that person that they completely changed their approach to their job and their feelings towards their employer?

This employee didn't go from A-Z overnight. There are almost always multiple signposts along the way, multiple points that have changed the trajectory of their career. We just failed to see it and manage it appropriately. We failed to establish, and more importantly, enforce, our expectations for standards of behavior.

And this is where the need for courageous leadership comes into play.

If an employee fails to meet your expectations, the first thing you must ask yourself is, "Did I clearly define and explain what I expect of them?" If not, you need to do so.

If you did, then you must have a crucial conversation with them. Identify the behavior in question. The behavior, not the person. This isn't personal. Focus on the specific situation, the background, the behaviors, and the impact their behavior is having.

Then work to create a supportive atmosphere by being approachable, authentic, and sincere, and allowing them to talk about it first, from their perspective. Remember, this is a conversation, not an interrogation, and your demeanor, questions, and tone should reflect it as such.

Oftentimes, this conversation alone will bring the root cause of the behavior to the surface, and the solution will present itself.

And if not? Offer them the opportunity to take responsibility for their actions in a way that allows them to maintain their dignity and without the need to feel ashamed. Vistelar co-founder Gary T. Klugiewicz offers this recommendation.

Ask the employee:

1. Did you simply forget to do what you were trained to do? If the answer is no, then ask:
2. Do you need more training? If the answer is no, then ask:
3. Did you knowingly and willfully refuse to do what you were trained to do?

Their answers will guide you to the next best course of action. By implementing an approach and a process like this early, and by consistently applying it, your employees will learn what to expect from you. Your job as a leader is to be predictable! You must be a thermostat in your environment, not a thermometer. Truly, your bearing—the way you show up each day—will affect the voice, input, and motivation of your team.

Giving Voice

Leaders are often ill-equipped to manage behaviors or respond to outspoken employees. However, you must ensure you create a supportive environment where everyone has a voice by learning to skillfully invite others to speak.

Your job as a leader is to be predictable! You must be a thermostat in your environment, not a thermometer.

Consider this insight in responding to employee activism:

Disregarding employee activists may be the equivalent of ignoring the canary in the coal mine: it could be a sign that managers can't hear things that don't fit with the established agenda. Hearing differences and being curious are vital to innovation and agility—and to hiring and retaining a new generation of talent that demands to be heard. Engaging with workforce activism has implications for every level and type of organizational leader and manager. Serious and sustained engagement with this issue has to be based on a new set of assumptions about who has a voice in setting organizational priorities - and how truth is spoken to power.

From the MIT Sloan Management Review: Brene Brown Podcast *"Leading in an Age of Employee Activism"* with Megan Reitz and John Higgins

Ultimately, strong leaders foster an environment and create relationships based on respect. The number one most important element of corporate culture as it relates to employee retention is that employees feel respected. (Sull & Sull, 2021)

Employees want to know that what they think—and what they have to say—matters. They want to know they are valuable members of a team, and they want to contribute. Allow others to speak up and tell it how it is. If you don't, bad practice in the workplace will not only become allowable; it will become the standard. Creating an environment where it is psychologically safe for employees to speak up will foster team building, trust, innovation, and inclusivity, in addition to improving accountability, adaptability, resiliency, and retention.

Oftentimes, managers and leaders insist they have created an environment to solicit feedback, stating they have "an open-door policy." But have they truly created a welcoming environment by remaining in their office? An office, or space, that is likely seen as intimidating to others? They say they are tired of "asking for people to speak up." Then perhaps they should spend more of their time and energy on listening and learning how to help people feel safe.

I've met leaders who tell me 'they' need to speak up more. 'They' need to be more assertive and courageous. Rather focus on creating an environment where they don't have to be so brave in the first place. For example, there's a great deal of difference in trying to have a conversation with someone in a group meeting versus taking somebody for a walk outside in the park. You'll get a very different quality of conversation depending on what you do.

From "*Activism at Work: Leaders Who Want Genuine Feedback*," Megan Reitz

Research has shown that the more senior you are, the more likely you are to believe that your people are speaking up, when in fact, they are not. This is called the "optimism bubble." (Reitz & Higgins, 2020) Challenge this assumption and the propensity to only listen to those who are "like-minded." Work harder to listen and be inclusive of those who voice opinions or experiences that are different from yours. One of the most important elements of corporate culture, as it relates to employee retention, is having supportive leaders who are encouraging and responsive, who listen, and who have their employees' backs. (Sull & Sull, 2021)

Step Two: Assessing Community Readiness

The second step in creating a culture of shared social responsibility is assessing community readiness, or the capacity of a community to accept and implement programs, policies and/or other changes that are designed to reduce lateral violence or abuse. Community readiness is a promising model for community healing and creating change. (Edwards, Thurman, Plested, Oetting, & Swonson, 2000)

For any form of social norming or cultural reframing to occur, the community has to be ready to accept the new norms. Social norms are specific to particular groups, as each group creates its own standards for what attitudes and behaviors are acceptable and desirable.

We tend to do what everyone else is already doing. Norms can be explicit or implicit, and their power comes from the social penalties of noncompliance or the social benefit of conforming.

Stages of readiness range from:

- Community tolerance: Having no knowledge or belief that behaviors are harmful.

- Denial: Having a vague awareness.

- Preplanning/preparation: Preparing to address an issue.

- Initiation: Creating a plan.

- Institutionalization or stabilization: Implementing the plan or processes.

- Confirmation: Expansion and professionalization of the new norms.

The attitudes, beliefs, and readiness of your organization can be gauged through assessments and surveys, such as engagement, climate, culture, and safety surveys.

"Never doubt that a small group of thoughtful, committed citizens can change the world; indeed, is the only thing that ever has."
– Margaret Mead, American cultural anthropologist

Step Three: Building a Primary Prevention and Behavior Change Platform

The third step in creating a culture of social responsibility is building a platform for behavior change. This starts with living and breathing your core philosophy. At the company at which I work, Vistelar, we teach to treat people with dignity by showing respect, and operationalize how to show respect by using empathy.

Empathy is the foundation for treating people with dignity by showing respect. To operationalize empathy:

1. Gather information to accurately identify your own and their thoughts and feelings.

   • Take their perspective (imaginatively put yourself in their place; apply the Empathy Triad).

   • Seek to understand (use beyond active listening skills, such as asking clarifying questions and paraphrasing).

   • Acknowledge their perspective (*"Thanks for sharing that with me, now I understand."*)

2. Anticipate their needs (try to consider what they might be thinking or feeling given the circumstances).

3. Take action (show respect and demonstrate concern via your proxemics, non-verbals, para-verbals, and word choice).

Sometimes even just appearing empathetic can reduce the tension in the room and de-escalate the emotions in others. It is about looking professional, demonstrating concern, and keeping everyone as safe as possible.

Many times, employees are unaware of their employer's core philosophy and core values and are unable to recite them. If they don't know them, how could they possibly act on them?

Many times, employees are unaware of their employer's core philosophy and core values and are unable to recite them. If they don't know them, how could they possibly act on them? Mission statements and core values must actually mean something. They must be far greater than just "words on a poster," and they must be translated into action. They have to represent who you are (as an organization) and what you do, day in and day out. Every team trains, educates, and prepares. It's not just that your team does those things; it's at what standards you choose to do them.

Every job is a self-portrait of the person who does it. Autograph your work with excellence.

Your platform for behavior change will be further reinforced by implementing a conscious-raising media campaign that reinforces the expectations of the new core philosophy. A multi-modal (advertisements, flyers, posters, table tents, emails, videos, training sessions, etc.) media campaign will raise awareness and reinforce the desired new norms. Covering how to develop a conscious-raising media campaign is beyond the scope of this book. However, Vistelar offers additional training in this area (for additional information please reference the section titled "Who is Vistelar" at the end of the book.

Your messaging must appeal to your employees' current thoughts and beliefs, meaning it must take into account your climate survey data so that it will relate to the target audience as much as possible. By launching and maintaining an awareness-raising and behavior change campaign, you will generate community buy-in (internalization) and, eventually, institutionalization of beliefs reinforced through policy.

"Powerful and sustained change requires constant communication, not only throughout the rollout but after the major elements of the plan are in place. The more kinds of communication employed, the more effective they are."

— DeAnne Aguirre, senior partner at Strategy&
and change management expert

Social Accountability and People Policies

With awareness and increasing buy-in, consider how the power of commitment could reduce or prevent undesirable behaviors. It is no coincidence that many of the strongest companies instill their mission and core values as part of their organizing principles.

Many companies and organizations have also effectively implemented:

- Acceptable behavior contracts (also known as an ABC policy).

- Expectation contracts.

- People policies.

- Code of conduct policies.

- Social accountability policies.

- Commitment to community pledges.

- Committees on civility.

All of the above pledges, contracts, and policies are designed by employers to reinforce their mission and the behavioral expectations of their employees. In essence, they are putting policies in place to reinforce their expectations and create a social contract based on civility, but for it to work, those expectations must be clearly defined, widely accepted, understood, and enforced consistently.

"Inconsistency is the enemy of peace."

— Joel Lashley, author of *Confidence in Conflict for Healthcare Professionals*

Step Four: Creating a New Social Contract

The fourth and final step in creating a culture of social responsibility is to create a new social contract.

In any environment, even in a church or a toy store, violence may occur. Still, everyone intuitively understands that some environments are more compatible with violence than others. That notion simply acknowledges that fights are more likely to break out at the corner tavern than at your local library—we all get that. Ultimately, the amount of violence that occurs in any setting depends on its established social contract. And that social contract is also what shapes the organization's response.

Only when we embrace a new belief system about violence can we begin to form a safer and healthier environment.

Proper policies, procedures, and training can establish and maintain a social contract that excludes violence, generates collaboration, supports more peaceful and attractive environments of care, and results in better outcomes. It all starts with professionals believing and expecting that violence is unacceptable.

Many times, people work harder to avoid conflict rather than face it head-on, causing even more problems for the employer. Training staff at all levels ensures that employees share the same goals and approach conflict consistently and supportively.

Of course, it is not easy for a group to decide what behaviors are tolerable, as behaviors tolerated by one social group may be abhorrent and disrespectful to another. The primary goal of identifying and establishing a new social contract is to:

- Create and maintain a safe and respectful community.
- Define a core philosophy that is actionable and professionally healthy.
- Create a system of support.

- Promote awareness about individual differences and beliefs.

- Educate about inclusion (in all forms).

- Educate about components of respect.

Social movement theories suggest that in order for a change movement to be effective, or in this case, in order to change the social contract amongst a group, leaders will need to:

- Transform perceptions,

- Legitimize the movement,

- Prescribe specific courses of action,

- Mobilize for action, and

- Sustain the movement.

The following tips will help you implement an effective social movement, in this case, the creation of a new social contract:

1. Create the expectation and make an agreement that everyone must take appropriate action whenever antisocial and violent behavior is observed.

    Adopt a "see something, hear something, do something" mentality when it comes to violence. Employees must be trained to consistently address the gateway behaviors of violence when they see and hear them, then take appropriate action. They also must learn to judge whether to take action with their co-workers and when it's necessary to call security or law enforcement.

2. Adopt a clear and broad definition of violence.

    Because violent behavior is connected through gateway behaviors, we need to include anti-social and threatening behaviors in our definition of violence, as discussed previously. Also, the refusal to follow basic policies and procedures should not go unnoticed and unanswered, even if we don't directly identify such resistance as violent behavior. If we can't get someone to comply with something as seemingly insignificant as wearing a visitor's pass, how do we expect to persuade them to cooperate when the stakes are even higher?

At the very least, a clear definition of inappropriate and violent behavior should always include behaviors that disturb or offend others, such as: demeaning language or comments regarding a person's race, religion, sexual orientation, age, body shape; profanity, swearing or cursing; shouting, yelling, or loud talking; implied or overt verbal threats; sexual comments and unwanted advances; touching without permission (unless necessary for the safety of self or others); behavior that disturbs others or causes fear.

3. Train employees to perform non-escalation skills.

Non-escalation is a unique skill set that precedes the need to use de-escalation tactics. By treating all people with dignity by showing respect, being approachable, and being mindful of our communication alignment, we can ensure that we are not unnecessarily escalating a situation.

4. Train professionals and staff to perform de-escalation and crisis management skills.

By training staff to recognize the signs of lateral violence, we can arm them with the decision-making skills needed to make safety assessments, de-escalate, or intervene if necessary.

For example, in the Vistelar *Crisis Management and Cognitive Challenges* training programs (for more information please reference the section titled "Who is Vistelar" at the end of the book), participants are taught to model calmness, reduce stimulation, separate and support, adapt communication, and meet unmet needs quickly and safely in order to de-escalate people in crisis. Untrained or insufficiently trained people tend to do what comes naturally when they attempt to de-escalate people in crisis. And what they naturally do is get too close, talk too loudly, talk too fast, and say too much. The above-mentioned strategies are helpful in de-escalating situations, whether a person is in crisis or not.

5. Adopt a zero-tolerance policy for violence and clearly define zero-tolerance.

   Zero-tolerance does not mean that we throw everybody out who yells or curses at work. However, it does mean that we consistently identify and address issues, like cursing and yelling, when they are first observed. If we can't effectively and reasonably rein in uncooperative, anti-therapeutic, and antisocial behavior, then clear consequences have to be presented and enforced. When we are threatened or attacked, those consequences have to be clear and enforceable.

6. Train to persuade and educate using evidence-based practices.

   Persuasion can be used anytime you encounter verbal resistance and seek a change in recognizing or changing behavior, and it will be covered more in-depth later in the book.

7. Make clear to everyone their right to protect themselves and their responsibility to respect others.

   Many human service workers honestly believe they do not have the right to protect themselves or their clients because they've been told throughout their career never to touch a client without permission—no matter the circumstances. This belief is obvious nonsense to some professionals, but it's an absolute truth to others.

The right to self-protection is an inalienable human right, and no state can make a law taking it away. Although many institutions have flirted with the issue, no hospital, nursing facility, group home, or other employer can enforce a policy that infringes on an individual's right to self-defense any more than they can ask them not to breathe! Also, no one can avoid the responsibility to protect people in their care or custody. Sometimes that means the need to "go hands-on," or to physically stabilize someone displaying at-risk behavior. What should medical workers do if their patient is about to swallow a bottle of pills, just watch? Ask some medical workers that question, and you may get some surprising answers.

The Continuum of Care

The Continuum of Care was originally developed by Covenant Health Plan for their *Interventions for Patients with Challenging Behaviors* instructor class. The continuum represents a care and intervention structure that integrates and includes the organizational community at every level, so it is a natural fit for an organization working towards creating a culture of shared social responsibility.

It has been adapted here to serve as an example of a fully integrated model of care. It serves as a way to operationalize a just culture or an explicit commitment to the community by:

- Acting with integrity and showing respect for ourselves and one another.

- Accepting responsibility for individual actions.

- Supporting and promoting collaboration.

- Demonstrating concern for the well-being of others.

- Promoting the benefits of diversity by practicing and advocating openness, respect and fairness.

The following list serves as organizational guidance when seeking to establish a commitment to creating community culture:

- Establish a core philosophy, such as treating all people with dignity by showing respect or service excellence.

- Create a foundation of support, starting with executive leadership and administration.

- Establish a caring watch, including all employees.

- Enable employees with the knowledge, resources, and clearly defined expectations and consequences.

- Empower employees with permission to act and by maintaining the confidentiality and integrity of internal reporting systems.

- Encourage employees with reinforced messaging. Encourage ethical decision-making, recognition of implicit biases, and weighing outcomes.

- Exemplify, leading by example and ensuring the consistent review and application of policy.

- Offer early support, at all levels, treating all people as individuals and working to reduce inequalities.

- Use emergency override situationally. Recognize that the capability of people falls on a spectrum of either high/low ability to act and high/low willingness to act.

What is Ethical Intervention/Emergency Override?

We are all human. Every now and then, we may have a bad day. Personal stress, lack of sleep, family pressures, and financial troubles can wear our patience thin.

Therefore, you will likely face situations where a colleague is heading in a direction or, perhaps, taking an action they will regret, or that will have negative consequences.

In such circumstances, you should consider making an ethical intervention. There is no such thing as an "innocent professional bystander."

As a professional, when you see inappropriate behavior by a colleague, you need to take action.

The need for an emergency (or ethical) override is a form of professional intervention. Professional intervention requires that we:

- Assist fellow community members.
- Fix something if it is going wrong.
- Stop something that is wrong.
- Report to the proper authorities and document appropriately.

There are three types of ethical interventions:

1. **Pre-incident prevention.** This begins with what people expect of you based on your past behavior (think: your ethical presence) and is applied as a verbal intervention implemented before the point of no return. For example, reminding someone that it's "showtime" or stating, "Hey, that's not what we're about here. We can do better."

2. **Direct-contact override.** Stepping in to take over the interaction, using the appropriate level of override.
   - Level 1: Verbal. For example, saying, "Jim, let me ask a few questions here while you go take that call."
   - Level 2: Positioning. For example, getting between your colleague and the subject and, if necessary, moving your colleague out of the way.
   - Level 3: Physical. For example, physically removing your colleague from the scene, if necessary.

3. **Delayed post-incident remedies.** If an incident occurs, doing the right thing following the incident (e.g., apologizing where appropriate, debriefing the incident

to improve future performance, notifying a supervisor, writing up the incident).

Remember, if you ignore a colleague's inappropriate actions, you are not only condoning them, but also potentially damaging your relationships with others who have the expectation that you will support them.

More information regarding the strategies of when and how to intervene is covered in the bystander mobilization sections of this book.

How Building a Culture of Shared Social Responsibility Improves Retention

Employees who are subjected to toxic, hostile, or laterally violent work environments often feel like the only course of action available to them is to quit. For their sake—and for the good of the organization—that should not be the only viable option.

Changing the culture is likely the most effective way to ensure employees truly feel they have alternatives to coping with such a scenario.

However, by employing the above-described strategies and the below-listed actions, you can work to improve employee retention. Franklin A. Shaffer (the president and chief executive officer at CGFNS International, Inc.) and Leah Curtin (the executive editor, professional outreach, for American Nurse Journal) believe that employers and managers can take several immediate actions to improve retention:

- Improve communication between administration, management, and staff. If rudeness, lies, stonewalling, gossiping, bullying, and other forms of negative communication are tolerated, good employees will leave.

- Hold employees accountable for fulfilling their job descriptions and standards of practice. Teach managers how to give feedback and reward them for doing it regularly and honestly.

- Heed the adage, "hire slowly and fire quickly." Teach managers how to interview and hire employees. Hire and train for civility.

- Deal expeditiously with conflict. Competent people want to work with other competent people in organizations that value and support their talents. They'll leave if those standards aren't met.

- Focus on fairness. Humans are wired to appreciate fairness. Employees who come to work on time and produce as expected don't like it when coworkers aren't disciplined.

This list was originally published in their article, "Nurse Turnover: Understand It, Reduce It," in the American Nurse Journal. (Aug 10, 2020)

Finally, consider providing opportunities for lateral job moves. Lateral career opportunities are 12 times more predictive of employee retention than promotions. (Sull et al., 2022) Not every employee wants to "climb the ladder" and take on additional work and responsibilities. A lateral move may be just what they need—an opportunity to learn more without the additional stress of a promotion. It would allow them the opportunity to have a fresh start with a variety of new challenges and a new team of people, rather than having to face the decision to quit and leave your company altogether.

Key Takeaways

- Work to build a culture of shared social responsibility by:
  - Mobilizing the strong opinion leaders.
  - Assessing community readiness.
  - Building a behavior change platform.
  - Creating a new social contract.
- Creating a new social contract will only be effective if you:
  - Transform perceptions,
  - Legitimize the movement,
  - Prescribe specific courses of action,
  - Mobilize for action, and
  - Sustain the movement.
- You can accomplish that through seven actions:
  - Create the expectation that everyone must take appropriate action whenever antisocial and violent behavior is observed.
  - Adopt a clear and broad definition of violence.
  - Train providers and staff to perform non-escalation skills.
  - Train professionals and staff to perform de-escalation skills.
  - Adopt a zero-tolerance policy for violence and clearly define zero-tolerance.
  - Train to persuade and educate using evidence-based practices.
  - Make clear to everyone their right to protect themselves and their responsibility to respect others.

Jill Weisensel

PART ONE CONCLUSION

So far, you have learned that you play a crucial role in creating a safe workplace environment—one that you will be proud to be a part of and one that you will feel physically and emotionally safe in.

Now I want to provide you with the knowledge, skills, and abilities to:

- Prevent lateral violence via the practice of "non-escalation."

- Be situationally aware.

- Recognize and correct gateway behaviors and other conditions that lead to lateral violence.

- Identify pre-incident indicators that can be a precursor to violence.

- De-escalate and recover from situations that could lead to violence at the point of development.

- Act appropriately when faced with violence and word-based methods fail.

The first part of this book focused on what lateral violence is and why we must work to end it. The second half of this book will focus on what you can do to stop it, and how you can do so safely.

Jill Weisensel

PART TWO
Professional Intervention

....

CHAPTER FOUR
Bystander Mobilization (Part One):
To Empathize is to Civilize

"The world is a dangerous place to live; not because of the people who are evil, but because of the people who don't do anything about it."

– Albert Einstein

Now that we better understand lateral violence and how to establish a new social contract (the why and the what), we need to shift into understanding "the how." To put a standardized code of behavioral expectations into action, you will need perspective (through perspective-taking).

Simply put, perspective-taking is the ability to understand how a situation looks and feels to another person. Perspective-taking is empathy creating, and empathy creates altruism (selfless concern for the wellbeing of others), whereas empathy is the ability to understand and share the feelings of another.

The uniforms we all wear or the titles we hold come with various expectations of expertise, competency, consistency, and credibility. But those expectations also come with preconceived notions and stereotypes, and with stereotypes, we have varied attitudes, beliefs,

73

perceptions, and biases.

In order to transcend the "isms" of racism, sexism, classism, ageism, ableism, and heterosexism, we must use perspective-taking: the act of perceiving a situation or understanding a concept from an alternative point of view, such as that of another individual.

Bystander Mobilization

Why focus on bystander intervention and mobilizing the "bystanders?"

Many people think of a bystander as someone who is present at the scene of a potential incident. Part of the confusion is how the word "bystander" sounds; it sounds like it means someone who is standing by. It actually is used to describe anyone who isn't either a perpetrator or a victim in a given situation, but is in a position to intervene before, during, or after the act. Or a member of a peer culture that contains abusers or victims. Or an authority figure in a position to enact prevention strategies. In that sense virtually everyone is a bystander. The critical question is, are you an empowered/active bystander or an inactive/passive bystander?

- MVP Strategies, NSVRC "Engaged Bystander" Interview with Jackson Katz – Part One, April 29, 2011, by Joan Tabachnick

Studies show that bystanders are present in up to 85% of "potentially risky situations" in everything from bullying and verbal abuse to lateral violence, and all the way to explicit sexual harassment, workplace violence, and sexual violence. Regardless of statistics, people who could prevent the event or make the situation end "better" are present more often than not. Bystanders are the largest group of people involved in the cycle of violence and represent a greater portion of the population. They greatly outnumber the number of victims or perpetrators in any given situation, and research has shown that workplace "bullies" are as likely to push out bystanders and witnesses as those who are being directly victimized. (Sutton, 2007)

Professionals encounter many situations where bystander intervention would be appropriate, including, among other things, bullying, discrimination, depression, alcohol use/abuse, and various forms of assault. One researcher found that when staff were subjected to verbal abuse by a colleague, bystanders did not intervene despite being present nearly 100% of the time. (Henderson, 2003) This further isolated the target and, in their silence, condoned the behavior. In more than 370 hours of observation of nursing units, Henderson never witnessed any acts or attempts of bystander intervention, despite knowing the benefits of doing so.

When surveyed, most employees believe that these types of situations could be avoided with "some type" of intervention, and most people indicate that they would "like to intervene if they knew how."

Concepts of bystander intervention and the need for ethical intervention are well understood in the realm of law enforcement, security professionals, campus crime prevention, and disturbance resolution specialists. They are less commonly understood by managers, supervisors, and organizational leaders outside of these practices.

It should be easy to "sell the need" for bystander intervention programs to people in positions of power, as people in positions of authority generally realize that they should act and that they have a professional responsibility to act (an explicit duty to intervene) because they are capable of acting (by having legitimate authority).

It is often more difficult to convince the average employee or citizen to intervene when they witness lateral violence and become aware of an inappropriate, wrongful, or potentially dangerous situation. There are many factors (above just assessing the nature of the behavior and whether it would be safe to intervene) that will determine whether or not a bystander will choose to step up and engage in the prevention of a potentially harmful situation.

Research has shown that arbitrary factors such as the potential victim's attractiveness, or the sex of the person being wronged, will impact a bystander's decision to act. Bystanders are often affected by their feelings towards the actor and the target, but their action (or inaction) should be based on the merits of the problem, not their relationship to the people involved.

More so, a bystander's decision to intervene will hinge greatly upon two factors: whether or not they feel a responsibility to act and whether or not they feel they are capable of acting.

Let's take a closer look at this. First of all, for the employee or citizen to feel a responsibility to act, we have to assume that they have a community-based belief system (a clearly understood social contract and strong personal value system) by which they live. Most people aren't generally motivated to do something for someone else unless there is a specific benefit or reward for them. Think of the "What's in it for me?" principle, also known as "WII FM... the radio station most people listen to." They will often weigh the perceived costs of intervening against the perceived impact of what could happen if they don't.

In the case of bystander intervention theory, very rarely is there a specific benefit for the person intervening other than for them to know that intervening is simply the "right thing to do." Banking on the belief that most people will act because it is the right thing to do is misguided.

More so, a bystander's decision to intervene will hinge greatly upon two factors: whether or not they feel a responsibility to act and whether or not they feel they are capable of acting.

Research has shown that when several people are present and recognize that a person needs help, the less likely it is that they will intervene. Most of the time, people assume "it is someone else's problem" or that "someone else will take care of it." This misguided assumption is driven by the socio-psychological phenomenon known as the "diffusion of responsibility," whereas people feel a decreased responsibility of action when others are present.

For many people, the problem in understanding bystander intervention strategies lies with the word "bystander" itself. "Bystander" literally means someone who is standing by, a witness to, but not participating in, and it is that understanding we are trying to move past.

Trying to mobilize people who are "standing by" is often a tough concept for people to wrap their heads around. For example, many people, regardless of their work context, witness social injustices such as racial slurs, promotional discrimination, defamation of character, or maybe even not-so-subtle forms of coercion. People who witness these things, and are aware of these behaviors, usually choose not to get involved by rationalizing that it has "nothing to do" with them and others appear unconcerned (the bystander effect).

"Bystander" literally means someone who is standing by, a witness to, but not participating in, and it is that understanding we are trying to move past.

It is easy to think of situations in which a person (who is neither the perpetrator nor the victim) observes an event and has the power to change the outcome for the better. However, bystander intervention strategies offer the tools needed for those observers to step in and positively alter the course of the outcome, both safely and effectively.

People also assume that since they are not engaging in the inappropriate behavior or are not the direct victim of the injustice, standing by seems like the safest and most neutral, non-polarizing option.

However, if you witness something going wrong, doing "nothing" is never a neutral option.

Quite frankly, doing nothing is making a choice in favor of the socially toxic behavior, further facilitating the creation of an environment that allows it. *If you do nothing, nothing changes!* Just because you don't take sides in a situation doesn't mean you have to remain neutral.

The error in this type of thinking is that when people witness negative actions, such as inappropriate water cooler talk, racist barriers to hiring and recruitment, or indignant treatment of subordinates, they are actually condoning the behavior they are witnessing. People often assume that ignoring the problem, or acting like they didn't see it happen, will make it go away. The reality is that ignoring the behavior does not make it go away, and just like a wound left unattended, the behavior actually increases in frequency and severity because the actors were tacitly empowered to continue.

However, if you witness something going wrong, doing "nothing" is never a neutral option.

Not only will your inaction empower the actors to continue, but you will have become complicit. Complicity means allowing the behavior or violation to occur, whether by enabling it to happen or by failing to report it. Complicity clauses are often included in the general code of conduct and organizational people policies. They can support the social contract by reinforcing both the need and collective responsibility for taking action.

Additionally, the confusion surrounding bystander intervention goes beyond the word "bystander." It also has to do with our understanding of the terms "victim" and "perpetrator." When we use the nouns "victim" and "perpetrator," we rigidly isolate and categorize people, events, and behaviors. These words are emotionally charged and come with a slew of subjective interpretations of what it means to "be a victim" or "be a perpetrator." Most of the time, this type of thinking allows us to minimize, rationalize, and write ourselves out of the equation because we don't categorize or label ourselves as fitting into one of those categories.

To approach this differently, we must stop using the terms as nouns and start understanding them as verbs. The term "victim" refers to only a small percentage of people; however, the number of those who have been "victimized" by the cycle of violence is much greater. For example, you may not have been a direct victim of sexual harassment, but you have likely been victimized by it if you have had to comfort and support a friend who was, or if your place of work was represented publicly as having multiple pending sexual harassment claims. Using that same line of thinking, I may not have been a direct victim of workplace bullying or harassment, but I have absolutely been indirectly victimized by it throughout the course of my career.

If we consider how the extended exposure to toxic workplace behaviors affect the lives of loved ones and coworkers, we start to realize that if we are not part of the solution, we could very well be part of the problem. By embracing this line of thinking, you will understand why people choose to intervene when they see things going badly. Make a choice to draw a line in the sand regarding the types of behavior you will allow in your presence, and participate in creating a living, learning, and working environment that is socially healthy for everyone.

By collectively mobilizing, engaging, and becoming intolerant of unacceptable behavior (no matter how small), we can prevent the escalation to more harmful and dangerous behaviors. Inappropriate behavior (think: disrespectful language, actions, bullying, predatory behavior) cannot survive in an environment that won't allow it. We need to create that environment in the workplace so that it's an emotionally safe and supportive place for everyone.

Why Don't People Intervene?

There are many reasons why people choose not to intervene in a situation, and most of them start with assumptions. Here are a few of the more prominent ones:

First, people assume a situation isn't a problem and fail to interpret the situation as needing help. Many people assume a situation isn't a problem because many laterally violent behaviors and tactics seem ambiguous. By utilizing risk and threat assessment skills and learning to identify red flag risk indicators, we will be better equipped to identify a situation as one requiring help.

By collectively mobilizing, engaging, and becoming intolerant of unacceptable behavior (no matter how small), we can prevent the escalation to more harmful and dangerous behaviors.

Second, people assume the situation is none of their business and fail to take personal responsibility. Even when bystanders do recognize a problem, most believe that it isn't their problem. This is where empathy and perspective-taking come into play. Perspective-taking is empathy creating, which leads to altruism. Bystanders must ask themselves, "What would I want someone to do for me if I were in this situation?" Generally, the answer to that question provides the bystander with appropriate actions.

Third, people assume someone else will do something. This is the diffusion of responsibility, whereby each bystander's sense of responsibility actually decreases as the number of potential witnesses increases. This simply means most people assume someone else will surely help because other people are there.

Fourth, people make the false assumption that other people aren't bothered by the problem.

People are generally afraid to inquire if there is a problem for fear they may be the only one who feels that way, and they don't want to risk the embarrassment if they are. However, statistics show that when one person steps up, intervenes, or inquires into an ambiguous situation, others often think and feel the same way. This is related to the spiral of silence: the fear of isolation or exclusion that consequently leads to people remaining silent instead of voicing their opinions. Most people are bothered by discriminatory remarks and harassment, but most people lack the communication and social skills necessary to appropriately address the behavior and alter the course of the outcome.

Finally, oftentimes people feel they don't know how to safely intervene because they don't have the proper skills to intervene.

By learning the skills taught in Vistelar's *Non-Escalation, De-Escalation, and Crisis Management* training, such as the concepts of showtime mindset, proxemics, beyond active listening, the persuasion sequence, engagement phrases, redirections, and trigger guards, bystanders are better equipped to confidently defuse conflict through conversation.

Additionally, by improving your threat assessment skills, learning bystander intervention strategies, and using engagement phrases (short phrases you can use that are non-judgmental and non-escalatory if delivered correctly), you will have the skills needed to confidently identify problems, mobilize your peer groups, and be prepared to better protect yourselves and others. Learn the skills, and seek out opportunities to practice them to build confidence, competence, and the moral courage to intervene.

One goal of this book is for you to learn the strategies, methods, and tactics to intervene both directly and indirectly and in both emergency and non-emergency situations. This book is not meant to cover all possible scenarios or variables but rather to create a foundation of life skills you can use anywhere, at any time.

Bystander Intervention in Action (Part One)

"I am only one, but still I am one. I cannot do everything, but still I can do something. And because I cannot do everything, I will not refuse to do the something that I can do."

– Helen Keller, American author

Bystander intervention theory (Dividio, Piliavin, Schroeder, & Penner, 2006) supports the following situational factors and psychological processes determining whether a person will be helped. (Latane & Darley, 1970) A breakdown at any one of these steps will result in no helping behavior.

In order to intervene or for bystanders to mobilize, people must:

1. Notice the event,
2. Interpret the event as requiring help,
3. Assume personal responsibility,
4. Know how to help/choose a way to help, and
5. Implement the help.

The following sections will go into each of these steps in more detail and include actionable skill-building strategies for each step.

Step One: Noticing the Event

1. Clearer (less ambiguous) and more vivid events are more likely to be noticed.
2. Excess environmental stimulation (distractions) reduces the likelihood that an event will be noticed.

Establishing Situational Awareness

Even if you have never found yourself in a life-threatening situation requiring split-second decision-making, you can still prepare and practice for the worst by practicing "when/then thinking." The concept of when/then thinking was developed by nationally known and respected law enforcement trainer "Coach" Bob Lindsey. When/then thinking is the process of visualizing and thinking through what you would do in a given situation, even if it's a situation you have never been in before.

In other words, when/then thinking is the skill of putting yourself into different types of scenarios so you can think through how you'd react to them *before* they happen. This is an important skill to have because it isn't a matter of *if* something negative will happen; it's a matter of *when*. This is related to the concept of perceived invulnerability. Perceived invulnerability is the (false) belief that since nothing bad has ever happened to you, nothing bad ever will. It is imperative to get past feeling "bulletproof" and recognize that situations and different environmental variables can make you more susceptible and vulnerable to adverse outcomes.

At the most basic level, situational awareness means paying attention to your surroundings and being ready to act when you sense danger. In other words, situational awareness is the practice of *when/then thinking* instead of *if/then thinking*.

If/then thinkers tend toward a rigid mindset of, "*If* something bad happens, *then* I will react."

When/then thinkers tend toward an agile mindset of, "*When* I sense danger, *then* I will respond according to a pre-planned, practiced response."

A pre-planned, practiced response includes these considerations:

- Verbal tactics (when, how, and what to say),

- Escape routes (how to leave, where to go, what to do when you get there),

- How to get help (who to call, what to say), and

- Physical alternatives (in what circumstances, availability of objects that could hurt or harm).

For example: If you close your eyes right now, would you know how many people are in the room and would you have a sense of their temperament? If there was a recent firing of an employee, would you know about it? If an employee started acting "out-of-character," would you take any action? If a stranger was in your building, would you notice? If they were carrying a backpack, purse, or satchel, would it arouse your suspicion?

Becoming a when/then thinker is the first step to improving your personal situational awareness. The next step is to gain a better understanding of your "personal level of awareness," which is, in essence, your overall level of alertness.

This also includes your overall understanding of the inherent dangers and resources available to you within your environment. Think of this as your own personal protection radar system.

Understanding Personal Levels of Awareness

To better explain personal levels of awareness, we reference world-renowned tactical trainer Lieutenant Colonel Jeff Cooper's "Color Code," which has been used by law enforcement and military instructors for many years to describe "escalating degrees of preparedness" and alertness at any given time.

While the Color Code model was originally intended for potentially combative and deadly force shooting incidents, public safety officials have universally adapted it as a gauge for all types of situations you may encounter.

The first condition of awareness is known as "Condition White." In Condition White, you are generally relaxed and, for the most part, unaware of what is going on around you and in your environment. Condition White is often referred to as a state of alertness equivalent to that of sleeping, meaning you are pretty much oblivious to everything happening around you.

Few of us intend to be in Condition White, but a lot of our behaviors can move us there. Being overtired, consuming drugs or alcohol, walking while texting, or walking with your headphones on are all things that can impact your ability to "take in" information from your senses that can give you an accurate assessment of how safe your environment is. Ideally, you should rarely, if ever, be in Condition White while at work.

The second condition of awareness is known as "Condition Yellow." In Condition Yellow, you remain relaxed, but you are now aware of who and what is around you. Think relaxed but alert. This simply means you are now paying attention to all of the sights, smells, and sounds that surround you. It means you have changed your level of alertness to recognize the actions of people around you, and you have started to casually think about how they could impact you and how you'd respond if something happened.

For example, if you were in Condition Yellow, you would start keeping track of people who were walking behind you and notice if they started following you when you turned a corner or entered a building. You would start to notice the sound of their footsteps quickening if they were trying to catch up to you while also looking for a close public or private place that you could enter quickly to get closer to people and away from danger.

Some other examples of Condition Yellow thinking include scanning for exits when entering a new building or picking a seat in a theater or restaurant that would allow you to keep an eye on who may be entering the building. A great practical example of when/ then thinking and Condition Yellow awareness is being mindful of the time so you can drive home safely on a Friday or Saturday night and get home before "bar close," which would increase the possibility of intoxicated drivers on the road.

The third condition of awareness is "Condition Orange." Condition Orange means you have again escalated your level of alertness from just being aware to being ready to act. In Condition Orange, you will be able to identify something of interest to you that may or may not prove to be a threat to you.

Whatever that "something" is that you have identified as a possible threat, you will remain focused on it and investigate it further to determine if it is a danger or not. If you identify someone or something that looks out of place or just doesn't "feel right," you should shift from 360-degree awareness to a more focused awareness of that danger, which will help you ascertain the true nature of the situation.

In the example above, if you suddenly realized you were being followed, you would start scanning for an area with more light, more sound, and/or more people and make a plan to head that way immediately. If you ducked into a convenience store or headed into a more populated area, you could find safety amongst others and see if the person following you was truly a threat. If they weren't, you lost nothing, but at least you put yourself into a better position if that person was a threat.

The fourth condition of awareness is "Condition Red." If you are scanning in Condition Orange and become aware of something you have confirmed truly is a threat, you will move into Condition Red, which is also understood as the "action state." In this state, you have specifically identified something you need to protect yourself against, and you will follow through with one of your mentally prepared when/then responses.

In the example above, you would have already changed your course from walking home and decided to stop inside the convenience store, but then you would go a step further and perhaps let the store clerk know that you believe you're being followed and ask them to contact authorities.

There is a final condition of awareness referred to as "Condition Black." Being the exact opposite of Condition White, Condition Black has often been referred to as the state of "blind panic." This would mean that something was happening to you or someone approached you that presented such a threat to your life that your body would immediately kick into a "fight or flight" response. Both Condition White and Condition Black are responses of untrained people, and training will help you overcome some of the barriers associated with the fight or flight response.

Condition Black renders you incapable of rational thought, and without proper training or sufficient experience, you would most likely "freeze" (or completely freak out) and be unable to respond to the situation. In our example above, if you were walking out of a bar at 2:00 a.m., slightly intoxicated and looking down at your text messages (Condition White), and you were suddenly followed, grabbed, and robbed at gunpoint, your mind and body would most likely kick into a Condition Black panic.

One of the things to remember about the conditions of awareness is that they are fluid. You can move from one condition to another multiple times a day or throughout a specific incident. It is possible to go right from Condition White to Condition Black (which could have catastrophic implications). It is also possible to be in Condition Yellow and hear something warranting concern, such as a woman screaming, moving you to Condition Orange or Condition Red, only to find out that the woman wasn't actually screaming out of fear; she was just shouting towards a friend who had forgotten something on the roof of his car and was driving away. This would move you back to Condition Yellow.

This is just one example of how you can move through the conditions of awareness and use the Color Code strategy to evaluate your level of alertness. Think of situations and examples of scenarios you have been in where this would have come in handy and perhaps helped the situation end differently.

Now that we have adopted the "scan and observe" mentality and understand the conditions of awareness, you also need to learn to trust your gut instincts. If something feels out of place or you feel like you could be in danger, you need to trust your gut. People often say they do not know what cues to look for.

We describe these cues as red flags, precipitating events, pre-incident indicators, or anomalies, which serve as risk indicators for things that could make you more vulnerable to certain behaviors. The better you are at identifying red flags, the better you will be at trusting your gut, identifying events requiring help or assistance, and avoiding potentially dangerous situations.

If you feel uncomfortable or unsafe, trust your intuition, do not enter a situation, and allow yourself to leave. Do not allow your sensory perceptions to get dulled by the day-to-day grind of work.

Establishing Baselines

Lateral violence doesn't just happen out of the blue. The path toward violence is an evolutionary one with signposts along the way. This is known as "leakage." When we review the entire sequence of events leading up to the last acts, we readily recognize a series of behaviors and events that lead down the path and set the stage for violence—those behaviors that offer clues into what was coming, such as conflict, broken relationships, antisocial behaviors, implied threats, social media postings, and explicit threats. We try to explain the spiral into violence as a simple cause-and-effect relationship, but it is not.

If someone had done something differently at a specific point in the timeline, the laterally violent outcome might never have happened. Hindsight is always 20/20 because it is easy to recognize the first acts of violence when we know how it ends.

In order to determine what behaviors are anomalies, we must first establish and understand the baseline. Your baseline behaviors are closely linked to the social contract in your organization.

You can establish and identify baselines of both environments and people.

For people, baseline behaviors are described as those that are typical to the person's natural personality, such as shy, grumpy, outgoing, or happy. This also includes understanding their backgrounds, such as their cultural upbringing, social development, and history of trauma. It also includes considerations of mental and physical health, cognitive disabilities, psychiatric disorders, or chronic pain. Their baseline body language should also be considered, such as if they typically project an image of confidence (comfortable, dominant) or inferiority (uncomfortable, submissive).

Once you understand a person's baseline, you can identify the anomaly behaviors.

An environmental baseline should mirror the environmental and behavioral expectations of the social contract. You need to identify the anchor points and habitual areas, the natural lines of movement, the proximal separation between groups that didn't come together and the separation between people who did. Break down body language in each phase to identify the baseline patterns.

Patrick Van Horn, the co-author of the book *Left of Bang*, explains it this way:

How does the place feel? Is it busy, or laid back? Is it hostile, or calm? Are people moving with a purpose, or simply taking their time and strolling along? How are people's emotions? Angry, calm, sad? These questions focus on atmospherics.

"How are people moving? Where are they coming from and where are they going? What paths are they taking? Do I see any proxemic pushes and pulls? From or toward what? These questions focus on proxemics.

Once you begin asking these simple questions, you can begin

establishing patterns. Once you identify patterns, any deviation from the pattern is a potential anomaly.

Look at every single object as a fact—a park bench, a tree, a sidewalk, a light post, etc. Once you understand the geographical layout of your environment, you can start making assumptions. Assumptions are the expected human behaviors or environmental factors.

Once you have scanned the area and made a list of facts and assumptions about every person, that is your baseline. When a person is not acting according to your assumptions, you have identified your anomaly.

Behavioral anomalies can be viewed on a timeline leading up to an event. Once you know what they are, you can work to avoid or change them. The thought is that by recognizing red flags or a cluster of behaviors sooner (staying "left" of the event), we can prevent or change the course of the action or outcome.

When evaluating anomalies and red flags, we must consider the frequency, duration, and severity.

Evaluate whether:

- Repetition increases (it occurs regularly).
- Duration (it becomes enduring).
- Escalation (increasing aggression).
- Power disparity develops.
- Attributed intent.

Red flag risk indicators vary depending on the environment. Think about the situations and places you will most likely find yourself in, and then look for and identify anomalies.

No one particular anomaly means you are in danger, but the totality of several may. Think about it like this: no one or two red flags should be considered in isolation. You should be assessing the totality of indicators and looking for clusters of them.

This idea can be conceptualized with the initialism "ABCDE."

Be Aware of the Baseline, look for the Change or Deviation in the baseline, and Engage (as appropriate or necessary).

Regardless of the type of incident, one of the things people often say after being victimized is "It just happened out of the blue!" However, that is almost never the case. In most cases, people outwardly "signal" their intentions well before it happens, we just don't always see, or look for, the signs. This phenomenon is no doubt a function of denial, again, rooted in the belief that nothing bad will ever happen to me because nothing ever has - and the problem may be even worse in caretaker and first responder professions as a result of the erosion of our perception of personal space.

To operationalize this in a real-life example, consider this bare-bones description of an environmental baseline:

You work for ACME Company. The main entrance to your workplace has a large lobby. Inside the lobby, there is a clearly marked welcome desk staffed 24/7. People are often coming and going, but there is a "visible ID" policy in place, so more often than not, everyone in the space is wearing an ID clipped to their shirt. Guests can check in at the desk and easily acquire a guest ID badge. The employee at the welcome desk is also responsible for packages—they sign for and accept packages nearly every day and put them behind the desk.

One thing you notice about the space is that it is clutter-free. Despite the number of people coming and going, you rarely see garbage in the space, and there are never any loose packages left lying around the lobby. At this point, you can assume that the employees care about the space being clean, and they care about not losing deliveries.

If this description of the lobby is accurate, then this is the description of your environmental baseline in that space.

But then, one day, you come to work and notice a random box

placed next to a wall. People are coming and going, but no one seems to be bothered by the random box.

The box, an unknown delivery, being unaccounted for and left in the lobby, would be considered an anomaly.

If then, over the course of the next few weeks, you see more boxes being left in the lobby unaccounted for, those anomalies now start becoming the new norm, or in these terms, the new baseline expectation for the space.

But something obviously had to happen for the baseline to change.

So, what happened? Was the normal employee working the desk out sick, and someone failed to explain the package policy to the replacement? Did the regular employee stop following the policy? Did the regular employee just stop caring about the policy? Any or all of these options (and there are probably many other assumptions we could make) could be possible.

However, applying this concept is critical in knowing what behaviors to look for and what behaviors or actions may require a second look. Consider this application: you know a particular employee to be hardworking, upbeat, always looking out for others, consistently going above and beyond to deliver exceptional work quality. They are friendly and approachable. They enjoy hanging out with co-workers on breaks and after work. Their workspace is always impeccable. This behavioral pattern over time describes their baseline.

Suddenly you notice their behavior change. Their workspace becomes cluttered and disorganized. They start avoiding coworkers on breaks and after work. They start responding to others in a way that is snippy and short-fused. Their behavior has now deviated from their baseline and you have identified the anomaly behavior.

Pre-Incident Indicators and Triggers

As mentioned previously, incidents of workplace violence rarely occur in a vacuum. When reviewed after the fact, pre-incident indicators are almost always present. Some incidents are the culmination of multiple warning signals over a period of time.

Examples of pre-incident indicators are:

- Gateway behaviors (shouting, cursing, name-calling, aggressive posturing).

- Known personal issues (e.g., relationship, mental/physical health, financial).

- Warnings from others about the behavior of an employee.

- Substance abuse (alcohol, legal and illegal drugs).

- Acts of aggression.

- Absence, tardiness, or requests for time off.

- Reduction in work performance.

- Signs of emotional distress or depression (isolation, withdrawal, poor concentration, crying).

- Habit of deflecting blame and responsibility; shifting blame to others.

- Excessive calls, texts, and voicemails.

- Frequent whining and complaints, inability to take responsibility.

- Journaling about or drawing violent acts.

- Recent acquisition or fascination with weapons.

If you notice pre-incident indicators, document and report them. Take appropriate action according to your organization's workplace violence policies and procedures. What actions are appropriate will vary greatly depending on your role in your particular workplace.

Beyond these indicators, there are also triggers that can set off a workplace violence incident, such as:

- Employee promotion, demotion, discipline, and/or termination.

- Disagreement between employees.

- Violations of a person's dignity (e.g., insults, humiliation, acts of prejudice) that can provoke retaliation or revenge.

- Emotional or physical threats causing fear.

- Stress from work demands, relationship difficulties, financial problems, emotional disturbances, pain, or mental disorders.

- Drugs and/or alcohol use.

- Bureaucratic and cumbersome procedures to resolve personnel issues.

Certainly, overt threats —whether verbal or written—should always be taken seriously. If you are exposed to such behavior, document and report the behavior and take appropriate action according to your organization's workplace violence policies and procedures.

Step Two: Interpreting the Event as Requiring Help (or Disruption)

1. Events that indicate more cues of another person's need are more likely to be interpreted as a situation requiring help.

2. Particularly in perceptually unclear (ambiguous) situations, the behavior of others will define whether help is required (given the bystander effect and the diffusion of responsibility, this could be misleading and problematic).

Don't fall into the trap of the bystander effect. Investigate the situation further, even if others appear unconcerned.

Ask others what they think about the situation (what was said or what you saw) and be visibly concerned. People do not speak up for peer discomfort for fear they may be in the minority. However, they are often part of the concerned (but silent) majority. Being visibly concerned will give others confidence in knowing they aren't "the only one feeling that way."

People may also resolve the "high cost for helping" versus the "low cost for not helping" dilemma by subconsciously reinterpreting the situation as one not requiring assistance. Remember, there are varying perceptions of what constitutes an emergency or non-emergency; what one person may consider an emergency, someone else may completely ignore.

To combat this, share your perspective; explain the behavior/ action/statement as you perceived it. Explain the impact you think those behaviors will have and suggest a solution. Oftentimes just setting the context and offering perspective ("perspective giving") is enough to offset the high internal cost for helping/low cost for not helping dilemma.

This will be broken down further later in the book, but all situations can be categorized as being either a non-emergency (no concern for physical safety) or an emergency (concern for safety or imminent concern for life). In either case, appropriate action, or the appropriateness of action, will vary depending on your training, experience, and role within your organization.

Key Takeaways

- Decades of research have shown that bystanders and witnesses are impacted by violence just as those who are directly victimized.
- Despite the impact to them, bystanders often fail to act or intervene, often because they're not equipped with the skills to do so.
- In order for someone to intervene and implement helping behavior, they must:
  - Notice the event.
  - Interpret the event as requiring help.
  - Assume personal responsibility.
  - Know how to help/choose a way to help.
  - Implement the help.
- Establishing situational awareness, understanding personal levels of awareness, and establishing baselines are important to determine when and how to respond to lateral violence.
- Lateral violence doesn't just happen out of the blue. Pre-incident indicators and triggers almost always serve as signposts along the way.
- Particularly in perceptually unclear (ambiguous) situations, the behavior of others will define whether help is required.

CHAPTER FIVE

Bystander Mobilization (Part Two)

Bystander Intervention (Part Two)

Up to this point, we have already covered several keys to bystander mobilization, including:

1. Noticing the event through situational awareness, determining baselines, and identifying pre-incident indicators and precipitating events.

2. Interpreting the event as requiring help by addressing ambiguity and conformity, the diffusion of responsibility and the bystander effect, and evaluating the concern for safety versus the concern for life.

Now we will cover the next three steps to bystander mobilization:

3. Assuming personal responsibility to help.
4. Knowing how to help.
5. Implementing the help.

Step Three: Assuming Personal Responsibility to Help

1. Don't rationalize away responsibility (diffusion of responsibility).

2. Social norms affect whether people feel they should help.

3. Explicit and implicit authority to help varies and impacts one's prescribed duty to help.

As mentioned previously, the diffusion of responsibility greatly reduces helping behaviors. It is easy to assume someone else will do something, and it is easy to say, "it's not my problem." However, the need to end lateral violence isn't about doing what is easy; it's about doing what is right.

> *However, the need to end lateral violence isn't about doing what is easy; it's about doing what is right.*

The world needs more helpers. Have a bias towards action; do not assume that someone else will handle it. In fact, assume someone else won't. Be the first, step up, and enlist others to help you. Verbalize your intentions to intervene, if safe and appropriate, and be specific, e.g., *"I will make sure they are okay and call medical if needed; please go find the maintenance technician and a supervisor."*

Additionally, social norms will impact whether people feel like they should help or not.

Social norms are often referred to as "informal rules that govern behaviors in groups." As I'm sure you've put together, social norms are inherent to the process of establishing a social contract. Social norms are central to the production of social order, as we all need to know what is expected of us and what the repercussions would be if we don't adhere. With respect to assuming personal responsibility to help, it is important to understand the influence social norms have on the group; helping others with no expectation of anything in return is altruism. A strong pro-social norm among the group will lend to more altruistic behavior because your in group is more inclusive.

Finally, people are more likely to take action when they are in positions of explicit responsibility (such as managers and supervisors) because taking action (or enforcing the rules) is implicit in their job role and is expected by others. However, throughout this book, the point has been made to encourage taking action, even without prescribed authority.

"You must never be fearful about what you are doing when it is right."
– Rosa Parks, American activist

Step Four: Knowing How and Choosing the Best Way to Help

1. Determine what knowledge or skills are necessary to intervene and identify if you have those skills.
2. People who are more knowledgeable about the situation can better evaluate alternative courses of action.
3. Other factors that influence helping at this stage include perspective-taking and engagement recognizing obedience to authority or perceived authority.

Helping others and intervening is not just about one decision. Failure at any step will result in no help, so we must also understand how social context affects individual behavior and an individual's decision to intervene.

Consider these barriers to helping:

- Individual variables such as personal knowledge or skills, confidence, and having a sense of social responsibility.

- Victim variables such as the appearance of the victim, friendship with the victim, perceived deservedness of the victim, and whether or not they will accept help.

- Situational variables such as the severity of the victim's need, the number of other bystanders present, the perception of the cost of helping, environmental conditions, and whether there is strength in numbers/other helpers present.

Research indicates that people are much less helpful or heroic than they think. The situational factors of a situation (such as the bystander effect or perceiving the costs of intervention as being too high, i.e., "I don't have time to help them right now. I have to go home and make dinner.") go the furthest in determining the likelihood of intervention.

The first thing you need to do is determine what knowledge and skills are necessary to intervene in a given situation. For something like a sexist or racist comment, you will need to have the ability to manage proxemics, appear concerned, create a supportive atmosphere, and sincerely deliver an engagement phrase to either the actor, the person victimized, or a supportive ally (all of these concepts will be covered in greater detail in the next chapter). If you have confidence in your ability to do all of those things, the likelihood of you helping in that type of situation increases.

Additionally, having sound threat and risk assessment skills will help you determine the best course of action and alternative courses of action. By conducting a threat and risk assessment of the situation, you will be able to evaluate what resources you have available, such as other staff members, equipment, or time. You will be able to determine if you should intervene now or in a different way at a later time (this will be covered in more detail in Step 5).

Step Five: Implementing the Help
1. People who have practiced the skills are more likely to intervene.
2. People who are well trained are more likely to help safely and effectively.

Bystander intervention skills are life skills, and there is no doubt that they need to be practiced. There are multiple ways to practice using the skills discussed throughout the course of this book, and it is imperative that you train with "fire drills," not just "fire talks," whereas you physically practice the skills and work to apply them in context - incorporating critical thinking and decision making. The two examples below are examples of "fire drill" type training options.

One way is to brainstorm conflict scenarios (by yourself or with others) and then identify the red flag interjection (or intervention) points. Once you've identified the points for intervention, write down possible solutions and possible scripts. You may be surprised at how many solutions you can come up with, especially when working with others. Oftentimes, when I run live bystander intervention training workshops, I may see 20 different solutions from 20 different people for one specific scenario, and the group is usually stunned by the perspective and creativity of others.

Another way to practice your intervention skills is to run through live training with realistic training scenarios. This type of training should be conducted with a team of people who have a strong understanding of the material. By walking through live scenarios, you can practice not only identifying the interjection points but also the skills of managing space, communication alignment, the delivery of engagement phrases, and the use of redirection and persuasion. The more you practice, the more confidence you will have in the skills, and the more likely you will use them.

Quick Tips for Taking Appropriate Action

1. If you notice an event out of the ordinary or observe a laterally violent behavior, trust your instincts and initial gut feeling.
2. Ask yourself, "Could I play a role here or is someone else better suited to respond?"
3. Assess your options to help.
4. Evaluate the risks. Look for low-risk options and decide to act now or later.

When talking about bystander intervention, people often think that in order to intervene, you have to perform some cape-toting superhero action. That could not be farther from the truth. Small interventions, either directly (in the moment and engaging with the person displaying the behavior) or indirectly (perhaps after the fact or by involving another or more appropriate staff member), will dramatically alter the course of the event.

Interventions fall into the following categories. As discussed above, assessing the type of incident you have will help you determine the appropriate course of action. Most incidents of lateral violence will fall into the non-emergency category, and will have both direct or indirect response options.

	Emergency	Non-Emergency
Direct		
Indirect		

Here is an example of using this simple quadrant in your decision-making process:

Imagine witnessing a coworker gossiping to another employee over their lunch break. You hear them make several inappropriate and inaccurate comments about a supervisor - specifically about how they handled a particular incident. You were involved in that incident and you know the gossipy comments to be untrue. At this moment, you have a couple of decisions to make. The first decision is whether to ignore the comments and walk away, or if you determine there's a need, to address it.

Given everything you've read so far, we are going to assume that you've made the decision to address it. Now you can choose to intervene directly in the moment, by engaging in the conversation and tactfully correcting the false information with one or both parties. This action would qualify as a non-emergency, direct intervention.

However, you could make the determination that intervening in that particular moment would be ineffective. As you've read previously, there are numerous reasons why you may not choose to intervene in the moment, such as you don't know exactly what to say or that you're concerned you may offend the person and become the target of untrue gossip yourself. So then, you could choose to indirectly intervene by addressing the comments made after the fact - either with the person that made them, with the person that they said them to, both parties, or perhaps another employee who may be better equipped to have the conversation. These would all be examples and variations of non-emergency, indirect interventions.

As you can imagine, different situations require different responses. There's an infinite number of ways we can work through them. Situations you encounter may not be as clear as the above example, but understanding and thinking through how situations play out will help you respond to situations in the future.

Case Study

"Dispelling the Myth: If you say something, it will make things worse."

By Joel Lashley, *Confidence in Conflict for Health Care Professionals: Creating an environment of care that is incompatible with violence*, 2015, P.2

This myth is probably the most damaging. We've all heard this one. Worse yet, some of us have probably come to embrace it on some level. So, if you have heard this myth, forget it. And, if you hear someone say it, correct them.

The fact is, if we ask someone confidently and respectfully

---

to stop behaving badly, they usually will comply. When we say nothing while people behave badly in our presence, the non-verbal messages of silence are permission and submission.

Specifically, if we say nothing when people threaten or even demean us, the non-verbal messages are, "It's okay to behave that way" or "I have no authority to act." Perhaps the worst of all nonverbal messages is, "I'm afraid." Failing to speak up when people need limits set on bad behavior usually ensures we'll get more bad behavior, and it will escalate.

If we focus on behavior, the attitude will follow. Skilled communicators focus on a person's behavior, not their attitude, which is important in developing a therapeutic relationship. What we naturally do is focus on a person's attitude, hoping their behavior will improve. This rarely works and can even backfire as the aggressor feels empowered by your attempts to assuage their anger by incessant apologies, allowing them to vent, and otherwise rewarding their bad behaviors. To make things worse, if all you have been trained to do is service recovery and/or crisis intervention, then appeasement is probably the only skill you have ever been taught.

Let's take a look at how this plays out in the following story:

The man had arrived at the walk-in clinic three hours ago and had already asked twice how much longer he was going to have to wait to see a doctor. He left work at lunchtime to finally seek medical care because nothing he had tried over the past three days seemed to be helping his abdominal distress. He tried to get in to see his family doctor, but no appointments were available that day, only adding to his anxiety. His wife kept calling his cell every 30 minutes or so to check on him

---

Case Study *continued*

and remind him that their daughter had a soccer game that afternoon. Finally, he was beginning to boil over.

"So, what's taking so long? Aren't you at a walk-in clinic?" she said sarcastically. "I thought you were supposed to just walk-in and get treated right away. Isn't that the point?"

"How should I know? They're busy, I guess," he replied.

"What about Ashley's game?" she asked.

"I'm sick! Do you really think I can go to that game tonight?!" he shot off angrily, feeling hurt by her indifference to his ailment.

"Well, I at least need you home to watch the other kids, so I can take her. It's an important game!" she shouted back.

"I just told you I'm sick!" he shouted into the phone. "All of her f*****n games are important! Why don't you just take the other kids with you?"

"I'm the assistant coach! How the hell am I supposed to watch them and coach at the same time?" she fired back.

"Oh, okay then. I'll just leave and be right home!" he replied. "And thanks for the concern! I could have f***ing stomach cancer for all you know!"

The receptionist made every effort not to make eye contact with the angry man on the phone and just went busily about her job. Then a nurse stepped out from the back and handed her some forms to process, paying no more attention to all the shouting and cursing than if it had been the hum of an air conditioner. To her, it was just another familiar background noise of the workplace, like the beeping of an I.V. pump.

Case Study *continued*

Finally, a lab tech stuck her head into the reception area and asked, "What's going on?"

"He's fighting with his wife," whispered the receptionist. The lab tech scanned the room and saw an elderly couple stand up. With his wife close on his heels, the elderly man scooted quickly behind his walker, intent on creating as much space as possible between themselves and the angry man. Some patients crawled deeper into their well-worn magazines, while others looked on disapprovingly. Others struggled to distract their children's attention from the angry man's shouting and profane language.

"Shouldn't somebody say something?" asked the lab tech.

"Tell his nurse," replied the receptionist.

The lab tech went back to the treatment area and quickly spotted the physician's assistant and one of the nurses huddling together over a medical record. "Do you hear that guy yelling out there?" she asked with a puzzled expression. "I hear him," said the physician's assistant. "Did the receptionist say anything to him?"

"Doctor Jenkins should probably say something to him," chimed in the nurse.

"He's kind of busy right now for that," replied the PA.

"In that case," replied the nurse, "I'll try and get one of these rooms cleared out as soon as possible so we can get that guy back here. He sounds like he's just angry about the wait."

"Good idea," said the PA. "Hopefully that will shut him up."

Hurt and angry, due to his wife's badgering and uncaring

Case Study *continued*

attitude, the angry man hung up on her mid-sentence. Then he stood and walked urgently up to the receptionist, yelling, "What the hell is taking so f***ing long?!"

For the first time, she looked up and made eye contact with the angry man, simply saying, "I'll tell your nurse that you're waiting."

So, what do we do next? Just as in the example at the beginning of this chapter, the bystander effect hinders the decision of who is responsible for acting. Therefore, we must begin by making it clear that it is everyone's responsibility to do something when an inappropriate behavior or potentially unsafe situation occurs, whether the actor is a fellow co-worker or a member of the public.

Then we have to give them the authority to act. In hospitals, when people act out, staff may feel even less able to intervene because of the mythology of healthcare violence discussed in Chapter Two. In training, we need to demonstrate how violence occurs and train staff to intervene as a team.

Bystanders generally know right from wrong but are unsure of how or when to take action to prevent a situation from getting worse. Most people think that intervention strategies require some drastic form of physical intervention; however, many appropriate strategies have very little to do with physical defense and have everything to do with communication skills.

All that aside, providers must understand when personal intervention isn't the safest or best option and when to seek help. In the event of physical contact, personal defense options will be required. These skills can only be developed through dedicated instructor-led training.

Nothing can replace well-trained providers and security personnel when one is seeking to prevent and mitigate violence. But even a well-trained staff needs policies and procedures that work together to reduce and prevent violence. If we're not all on the same page, we will continue to struggle with laterally violent behavior and its consequences and repercussions. The importance of communication and non-escalation/violence prevention skills, including bystander mobilization training, cannot be overestimated.

"For things to change. We must change. For things to get better, we must get better."

– Heidi Wills, motivational speaker and civility thought leader

---

Key Takeaways

- Have a bias towards action; do not assume that someone else will handle it. In fact, assume no one else will.
- The situational factors of a situation (such as the bystander effect or perceiving the costs of intervention as being too high, i.e., "I don't have time to help them right now. I have to go home and make dinner.") go the furthest in determining the likelihood of intervention.
- Intervention options can be categorized as direct or indirect, emergency (life-threatening) or non-emergency (non-life-threatening), and will vary depending on your training, experience, and role within the organization.
- Small interventions, either directly (in the moment and engaging with the person displaying the behavior) or indirectly (perhaps after the fact or by involving another or more appropriate staff member), will dramatically alter the course of the event.
- Appropriate intervention strategies often have little to do with physical defense and everything to do with communication skills.

CHAPTER SIX

Taking Action

The Art of Bystander Mobilization

The TAKES ACTION acronym, (which I co-developed) was created in response to the need for a comprehensive bystander intervention program rooted in applying "how to intervene" above and beyond just understanding why we need to intervene. The acronym is based on more than 40 years of social science research and is easily operationalized in any environment, for any situation.

The TAKES Acronym

The first part of this model is TAKES. It stands for *"Threat Assessment Keeps Everyone Safer."*

TAKES focuses on the importance of safely assessing situations to support a safe community.

The key to this all is being personally aware of your environment. Your ability to recognize situations requiring disruption will depend greatly on how ambiguous the signs are (red flags and anomalies) but will also hinge on how aware you are in that moment and in your environment (also refer to when/then thinking and conditions of awareness in Chapters 4 and 5).

For example, if you saw someone with a major injury, there would be no doubt in your mind that you would call for help. However, intervention is still needed in situations such as a coworker's absenteeism, depressed mood, or increased drinking behaviors, but it is harder to recognize.

It is important that when we recognize these signs, we take the time and effort to communicate with each other. It is much more important to identify and ask the difficult questions rather than ignoring the problem "hoping it will take care of itself." It will not.

Note that the company at which I work, Vistelar, teaches several tactics in its *Non-Escalation, De-Escalation, and Crisis Management* training program that specifically apply to the TAKES model. These tactics include *Be Alert & Decisive, Respond - Don't React,* and *Proxemics 10-5-2.*

The ACTION Acronym

The second part of the TAKES ACTION model is the ACTION acronym. It was developed to operationalize the ethical decision-making steps necessary to safely intervene.

Aware: Notice the event and interpret it as a problem. Identify red flags and assume personal responsibility to help.

Create: Create possible solutions. Think it through and pick the most effective strategy.

Take your time and tag team: Stay calm and slow things down. Enlist help if you can.

Intervene: Intervene when it is safe and appropriate. Timing is an undervalued element of communication.

Open dialogue, observe, and offer options: Be conscious of and deliberate with your delivery style. Use perspective-taking, set the context, and communicate in light of the desired outcome goal.

Negotiate a solution and negate further conflict: Draw a mental line in the sand and know the appropriate next step.

As discussed previously, determining what actions are appropriate will depend on your training, experience, and employment role. Your prescribed duties, intervention capability, organizational policies, and local laws will guide you.

Determining appropriate action will also include a cost/benefit analysis of:

- Personal biases (also consider: the ladder of inference).

- Identifying or developing alternative courses of action.

- Analyzing both short-term and long-term risks.

- Taking action with a commitment to accept responsibility for the outcome.

- Evaluating if the actions are likely to prevent future occurrences.

Threat Assessment and Environmental Risk Assessment

A lack of basic assessment skills is another issue that combines to create a laterally violent and violent culture in the workplace. We are generally poor at recognizing the cycle of violence. When we drive a car, we look ahead, to the sides, and occasionally behind us. We listen, we interpret traffic patterns, we look for danger, and we plan how to extract ourselves from danger. We also think about what measures we might take should danger spontaneously present itself. We should be conducting the same types of assessments in our work environments.

At its most basic level, a risk assessment can be understood as a systematic process of evaluating what risks you are vulnerable to. You need to be able to identify your vulnerabilities accurately so you know what risks you might face, and you need to be aware of the elements in your environment that pose threats to those vulnerabilities. To make it simpler to understand, consider it a hazard assessment of an area.

Threat assessment is the practice of determining the credibility and seriousness of a potential threat (whether something is an actual, inherent, or potential threat) and the probability that the threat will become a reality (determining the intent and capability of the threat actor). Consider it a hazard assessment of a person.

Threat assessment aims to interrupt people on a pathway to committing laterally violent or violent behavior. It is an objective, fact-finding process designed to identify, assess, and manage the risk of violence that a particular person poses.

In a given situation or of a specific person, threat assessment is a continuous process. It is not something you do "just one time."

The better we are at identifying pre-incident indicators or precipitating events (red flags), the better we will prevent or avoid potentially dangerous situations. These red flags are often identified after the fact, causing us to say things like, "Oh, wow, I should have seen that coming—all of the signs were there!" The goal is to identify these behaviors on a timeline—before, or "left" of, the event.

Over time, we become desensitized to toxic tactics and laterally violent behaviors because of our constant exposure to them. We start disregarding pre-incident indicators and become complacent with who we allow into our personal space. Many workplaces have formed a culture of denial that dismisses threatening behavior and fails to understand the negative impact of antisocial and uncooperative behavior.

The *Be Alert & Decisive* tactic (taught in the Vistelar *Non-Escalation, De-Escalation, and Crisis Management* training program), serves as the foundation for personal safety and overall readiness.

Be Alert is understood as what to look for. Become proficient in behavioral observation, situational awareness, and decision-making.

As Vistelar teaches, when you enter your area of observation, quickly perform a scan for any immediate threats, and get a feel for the atmosphere. In this case, listen for and look for anything that could cause emotional or physical harm to you or anyone else. Assess the body language and demeanor of those in the room. Be on the lookout for aggressive posturing, any weapons or potential weapons, or anyone paying more attention to someone else (or you) than to what they are doing. Start close and finish far. This is important because the closer a potential threat is, the less reaction time you have. Threats that are closer to you are usually a higher priority.

Then you must evaluate the totality of the circumstances.

We have to observe behaviors (individually) and then communicate and collaborate (with others) to share what we know. This will help you, as a team, in identifying clusters of behavior that warrant additional attention and potential action. This is why organizations have multidisciplinary and multi-agency threat assessment teams that share information freely. Generally speaking, no one person has seen all of the indicators, and working together will allow you to stay "left of bang."

Dispelling the Myth Case Study: "He just snapped!"

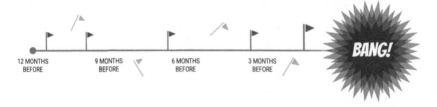

Tony worked for a large construction company driving heavy equipment. He had been working there for almost 30 years and was nearing retirement.

He was an exemplary employee. He always came to work early, stayed late, and produced the highest quality work. He had a great attitude, loved to laugh, and other employees enjoyed being around him. They all knew that if Tony were assigned to their team, their project would finish on time and on budget.

It didn't seem to matter how much extra work the foreman gave him; Tony would just get it done. He never complained. He never failed. He'd just make it happen.

Tony was well respected by his peers because, despite pressures to finish jobs on time, he always did them "by the book." He followed all the safety procedures because he knew it could be a matter of life or limb on job sites like his.

One day Tony and his team were assigned a very large project—a new factory built near the outskirts of town. Several very large pieces of specialized equipment were brought in, including a massive Transilift heavy crawler crane.

The operation of the crane came with many safety precautions, including things people don't often think about, such as requiring an experienced operator to operate, needing near-perfect weather conditions, and ensuring all major motorized components were inspected and signed off on at multiple points throughout the day.

Tony was the primary crane operator for the first several weeks on the job site and followed these precautions "to a T."

Unfortunately, the project started falling behind, and Tony's corporate office ordered additional help to assist with the build around the clock. Far less experienced employees were now on the job site, and Tony was very protective of them. He explained to the foreman that no one should operate the crane without a minimum of three years' experience as a crane operator.

But the foreman didn't listen and had someone far less experienced, Charles, start operating the crane when Tony wasn't there. Upset, Tony again expressed this as dangerous to his foreman. The foreman didn't change his decision. In fact, the foreman was more concerned about hitting the project deadline, so he started letting other safety precautions go, such as helmets, safety glasses, and the use of seat belts while operating company equipment. He felt those precautions were just slowing them down. Tony was upset but carried on. Charles called in sick one day, and the foreman asked Tony if he would come in on his day off. Tony told him no.

A few more weeks went by, and the employees on the site started to notice the quality of work going down. They realized that Charles wasn't experienced enough to complete the build, and it had become obvious that finishing the build on time was more important than building it well. While they were concerned, they weren't concerned enough to "bother" or "risk upsetting" the foreman.

Seeing this, Tony had had enough. He talked to the foreman one more time, who blew him off. Tony then reached out to the corporate office and cited numerous safety violations occurring on a daily basis and stated that "he couldn't bear to see any one of his team members hurt." Corporate was silent. They wouldn't return his calls (which were now daily), and they wouldn't respond to his emails (which were now weekly).

Tony was furious. He was furious and frustrated but internally torn. He was so close to retirement ... did he really want to ruffle all these feathers now?

A few days later, Charles had an accident while operating the crane in high winds. Multiple workers were injured, including Tony's best friend, who was injured the worst. Tony's friend was paralyzed from the waist down and unlikely ever to walk again.

A short while after the incident, numerous interested parties became involved in the investigation to determine what happened. Members of the corporate office made a statement that the incident was a "fluke," that "all safety precautions were followed as per statute," and that they had no wrongdoing in the matter.

Tony couldn't take it anymore.

Hearing this on the news and knowing it was a complete lie, he couldn't bear it. He felt personally responsible for the accident and for paralyzing his best friend. So he went to his office and started typing an email to the investigators. And he kept typing, and typing, and typing. The more he typed, the angrier he got. And finally, he got so angry that within seconds of hitting the "send" button, he picked up his entire computer and threw it out of a second-floor window. The computer crashed to the ground, and luckily, no one else was hurt.

Tony was fired the very next day.

When human resources asked his foreman about his behavior, he responded, "I don't know. I don't know what happened. He … he just snapped."

If you break this story down, piece by piece, you can easily determine the situational and environmental baselines and the anomalies. Looking at how it ended and working backward on the timeline, you should be able to identify numerous interjection points that would have kept this situation "left of bang" and likely saved Tony's career.

Proxemic Management

A key component of managing your personal safety involves not only evaluating and assessing your surroundings but also managing your space. We can manage distance by practicing proxemic management or the reduction of risk through proxemic shifts—adjustments made to increase safety in your physical space.

Proxemic management is a concept I developed to describe the skill of actively managing distance and space. Time and space are viewed as both an opportunity and a tactic.

Proxemic management enables you to take ownership of your space and empowers you to stay emotionally and physically safer within that space. It encourages you to be mindful, not fearful, of environmental conditions that could increase your chances of being victimized (regardless of the offense: harassment, theft, assault, etc.).

To stay safe, the space you need to control isn't just directly in front of you. It includes the evaluation of your complete 720-degree bubble to get a full picture of everything that is going on around you. It includes looking in front of and behind, left and right, and at everything above and below you. This includes assessing all the potential environmental factors that could enter and/or change that space.

Proxemic management also includes considering your position in relation to other people (also known as relative positioning) and assessing barrier options or exit strategies. Barrier options are things like tables, chairs, corners, pillars, escalators, and garbage cans: basically, anything that you can use to create a barrier, either permanent or temporary, between you and the other person (or potential threat) that will help you create time and distance from them, if you need to.

Also, consider the air temperature, the conditions of the walking surface, perhaps a low ceiling or a low hanging shelf, the number of people walking by, or how crowded it is. This also includes things like walls, doors, desks, and chairs and could include cars driving past, how fast they are driving, and if there is a stop sign nearby.

When it comes to understanding proxemics and space management, you have to get creative and really think about all the factors in that space that change your level of safety in it.

Here's a quick example:

If you were to go to your human resources office on any given day, most reasonable people would agree that it would be pretty safe to go there in comparison to going there on a day when multiple people were about to get fired or laid off. By going there on any "normal" day, you wouldn't run the risk of engaging with people having heightened emotions (particularly that of fear, anger, and rage) and therefore, having quite varied, unpredictable, and potentially volatile reactions.

So in this example, you could still choose to go to HR on the day of mass layoffs, but in evaluating the proxemics and the totality of the situation, the choice to do so is clearly less desirable and less safe than the other.

However, in the event you unknowingly walked into HR during a termination whereas the (now former) employee lashes out by screaming, crowding, shaking their fists at people, and issuing direct threats, you'd now have a tool you could use to manage your safety in the moment. The simplest, safest, and most effective answer would be to manage your proxemics by leaving the area.

If you're unable to leave, work to maximize the distance between you and the aggressor. If you're unable to maximize your distance, work to put a barrier (or barriers) between you and them - a desk, a cubicle, a pillar, or a wall. The barrier will not only help you create distance, but will also help conceal you from their view. If you're unseen, you're less likely to become the target of their anger, regardless if it manifests as a verbal onslaught or physical assault.

In the field of communication, proxemics refers to the study of non-verbal communication and how distance affects how we communicate with each other. It is the study of the cultural use of space. For the purpose of managing conflict, proxemics refers to where you are positioned in relationship to another person and how it impacts your ability to safely communicate, both verbally and non-verbally.

We encourage you to take ownership of your space and be empowered to stay emotionally and physically safer within that space. We encourage you to be mindful, not fearful, of environmental conditions that could increase your chances of being victimized.

Managing proxemics is about using position as leverage. Time and space are seen as an opportunity and a tactic: you choose what you do, when and where you can most safely do it.

Space equals time, and time equals options.

There is a subjective time-distance relationship (known as the reactionary gap) that can be used to determine reaction time based on distance. There's also an injury-distance relationship (known as the liability gap). There is a direct correlation between injury potential and the distance from a threat.

Space equals time, and time equals options.

The distance needed to stay safe from a threat can be measured by assessing the potential personal damage based on the available weapon system (hands/feet, pens, knives, clubs, firearms, vehicles etc.), the specific target (someone or someplace), and the scale of injury or damage.

Ultimately, understanding this space-distance safety relationship is pivotal to understanding de-escalation as it relates to space:

- Create distance: Engage in proxemic management.

- Buy time: Slow things down and create more space.

- Persuasion communication: Defuse literally, or diffuse the energy in the space using your communication skills.

The concept of proxemic management is incorporated into a tactic taught in the Vistelar *Non-Escalation, De-Escalation, and Crisis Management* training program named further *Proxemics 10 - 5 - 2*. This tactic operationalizes what you should be looking for and what you can do when 10, 5, and 2 feet away from someone.

No matter how you look at it or how you choose to define it, there is no denying the relationship between your safety and the distance you maintain from a potential threat.

Intervention Strategies

Throughout this book, we have made it clear that it is everyone's responsibility to do something when an inappropriate or unsafe situation occurs. However, the intervention strategy you choose to employ will be dependent on a number of factors. You must evaluate the totality of the circumstances and then assess the options available to you based on your training, experience, and comfort level. If you choose to intervene, choose the safest and most effective strategy that will maximize your strengths.

The strategies below were developed by multiple universities, including the University of Arizona, Virginia Tech, Syracuse, and Marquette University, and are compiled here to assist you in understanding all of the intervention options and creative strategies available to you that can apply across a variety of situations.

Presence

Sometimes your presence alone is enough to deter a situation. Think about surveillance cameras in a room; people will generally alter their behavior because they know they're being watched and could get caught. If you are known as a person who won't tolerate lateral violence, the likelihood of it occurring in your presence will decrease.

Presence as a strategy is also useful because it allows you to monitor a situation from a safe distance. This way, if you're unsure if a situation requires help, you can observe it and take mental notes of what is going on in case something does go wrong.

Here are a few additional elements of using presence as a strategy, originally developed by Vistelar co-founder Dave Young:

Acknowledge presence: The actor may not know you are there.

Confirm presence: You see the actor make eye contact or alter their behavior after seeing you.

Contact presence: You engage with the actor.

Verbal: You engage in conversation with the actor.

Barrier: You find or create a barrier between you and the actor.

Monitor: You monitor the situation from a safe distance.

Group Intervention

There is safety and power in numbers. The group intervention strategy is best used with someone who has a clear pattern of inappropriate behavior where many examples can be presented as evidence of their problem or unprofessionalism. This strategy is designed to let others know that they are not alone in their discomfort. For example, if a coworker makes several racist jokes, you might simply turn to the group and ask, *"Am I the only one uncomfortable with this?"* This creates options by allowing you to evaluate the situation and recruit the help of colleagues to determine the best course of action.

Clarification

People who verbally express negative attitudes towards others expect other people to go along with them, laugh, and join in. They do not expect to be questioned. By asking a question like, *"I'm not really sure what you meant by that. Could you please explain that to me?"* you create the opportunity for them to rethink the assumptions that underlie their statements and attitudes and also empower others to express their disagreement in a way that is not disrespectful.

Disagreement is okay; disrespect is not. Just because someone's opinion differs from yours doesn't automatically make them wrong. Two people can look at exactly the same thing and see something totally different. And that is okay.

Bring It Home

The "bring it home" strategy is designed to create perspective for whoever is acting in a degrading manner. It "re-humanizes" their target and makes them think about what it would be like if someone treated somebody they knew like that. For example, if someone makes fun of another employee, saying they're "completely incompetent" because they have Attention Deficit Disorder (ADD), you could simply say, *"Whoa, time out. How would you feel if your brother had ADD and someone talked about him like that?"*

"I" Statements

Think about how you feel when someone points the finger at you and says in an accusatory voice, "You really need to stop acting like that; you're embarrassing the family." Instead, "I" statements are easier to hear since they are about the feelings and thoughts of the person making the statement and not criticizing and accusing the other person. People are less likely to become defensive when using "I" statements. For example, you could say, *"I find it embarrassing when you act like that. I'd like it if you could change your behavior in the future."*

Humor

Humor is a difficult strategy as it can easily escalate if people feel they're being mocked. However, using humor effectively can reduce the tension inherent in the intervention and make it easier for the person to hear you. Be careful, though, not to be so funny that you undermine the point you're trying to make. In my experience, humor is best used as a strategy if you have a close or positive working relationship with someone. For example, if you overhear a coworker make a harsh or discriminatory comment about the percieved ability or competency of a new hire, and you could choose to address the comment by saying, *"Woah, now hey. You were new here once too and you turned out... ok."* If you delivered that engagement phrase with a positive and playful tone, and a wink or a smirk, that comment would likely get the point across in a non-escalatory way.

The Silent Stare

The "silent stare" or "the look" works very well if you connect it to parents, who have the ability to communicate their displeasure with their child's actions simply by staring or giving you "a look." No words even need to be spoken. Sometimes a disapproving look can be far more powerful than words. Think about a time when someone you really respected just looked at you and shook their head in disapproval. Remember how awful you felt? I sure do.

Distraction

The goal of distraction is not to directly confront the situation but rather to interrupt it and change its course. This is an especially useful technique where there is a higher risk of heightened emotions, like a heated work argument over a missed priority deadline. In this situation, you may have multiple people engaging and only one of you. Use a distraction, such as by saying, *"Hey, I think lunch is finally delivered,"* or *"I'm pretty sure the boss just walked in,"* to redirect the focus somewhere else or draw attention away from the argument.

"We're Friends, Right?" or "We've Worked Together a Long Time, Right?"

This strategy works best if you can take your colleague off to the side or if you can wait until later to address them. That way, you can avoid humiliating them in front of their peers and increase their likelihood of hearing and valuing what you say. For example, if you overhear a coworker saying something awful or untrue about another coworker, you can talk to them after the fact and say, *"Hey, we've worked together for a long time, right? I don't want to fight with you, but what you said about Tom earlier is actually untrue. I was there."*

Cut and Divide

The "cut and divide" strategy relies on creating space and physical separation between the involved parties. Recruit help if you can, as it is much easier to separate and support multiple people when you have additional people. Use sound proxemic management and communication skills to separate them. By separating them and getting them out of the eye sight or ear shot of the other person, you can help them cool off and prevent them from trying to posture or escalate in front of their friends. By having no "audience," they will potentially have less motivation to show off or escalate. Don't use this strategy where your threat assessment results in the potential risk of physical injury.

Take a Picture

The "take a picture" strategy encourages you to use your technology to your advantage. People immediately sensor their behavior when they know they are being recorded. Pretty much everyone has a camera phone, so it is now easier than ever to record good witness information. Notice a security camera? Politely point it out to the person acting up, and remind them that it's not worth getting caught.

Key Takeaways

- The TAKES ACTION acronym helps bystanders understand how and why to intervene.
- TAKES: Threat Assessment Keeps Everyone Safer.
- ACTION: Aware, Create, Take Your Time/Tag Team, Intervene, Open Dialogue/Observe and Offer Options, Negotiate a Solution and Negate Further Conflict.
- Threat assessment is the practice of determining the credibility and seriousness of a potential threat and the probability that the threat will become a reality. It aims to interrupt people on a pathway to committing laterally violent or other unsafe behavior.
- Proxemic management enables you to take ownership of your space and empowers you to stay emotionally and physically safer within that space. Time and space are both an opportunity and a tactic: you choose what you do, when, and where you can most safely do it.
- There are many intervention strategies. Evaluate the totality of the circumstances, assess the options available to you, and use the safest strategy that maximizes your strengths.

Jill Weisensel

CHAPTER SEVEN

Intervention and Engagement Skills

More often than not, the intervention needed in a laterally violent scenario will be low level (meaning, not physical). Therefore, bystander intervention moments are less often about what to "do" and more often about what to "say" and when.

One of the most undervalued elements of intervention and delivery is timing. You must first consider your headspace, their headspace, and if there is enough time available to have the difficult (but respectful) conversation.

The following engagement skills will help you intervene simply by communicating at an appropriate interjection point.

Consider and apply these foundational elements of delivery style:

- To whom you say it (your audience).

- What you say (the content, your word choice).

- When you say it (timing).

- Where you say it (the location).

- Why you say it (by presenting your evidence, reasoning, desired outcome).

- How you say it (your pace, pitch, tone, inflection).

- How you look (non-verbal communication).

People generally remember the impact (how you made them feel) instead of your intentions (regardless of how well-intended you were).

Remember, it is not just about what you say; it is about understanding what you are trying to do with what you say or the outcome you're looking for. People generally remember the impact (how you made them feel) instead of your intentions (regardless of how well-intended you were).

At the point of impact, it is possible that the other person will react irrationally. During times of irrationality, we tend to focus more on non-verbal behaviors, so your non-verbal messaging may be all that gets through. This is why communication alignment is critically important.

Non-verbal communication plays five roles:

- **Repetition**: It can repeat and often strengthen your verbal message.

- **Substitution:** It can substitute for a verbal or oral message. For example, your facial expression often conveys a far more vivid message than words ever can.

- **Complementing:** It can add to or complement your verbal message. As a boss, if you pat an employee on the back in addition to giving praise, you may increase the impact of your message.

- **Accenting:** It can accent or underline a verbal or oral message. Pounding the table, for example, can underline the importance of your message.

- **Contradiction:** It can contradict the message you're trying to convey, thus indicating to your listener that you may not be telling the truth. For this reason, you want to avoid non-verbal gestures that contradict your intended message.

In addition to the information above, it is crucial to understand that any nuance in your rate of speech, pitch, volume, or tone will give those sentences different meanings. For example, the inflection or tone you put on a word will reflect your attitude, opinion, or bias, potentially converting a sentence from a gesture of support to insulting.

Use professional language to achieve a professional objective. It is the shorter report way, the lower liability way, the fewer lawsuits way, the higher retention way, and the more humane and ethical way.

The Language of Engagement: Using Word-Based Methods to Intervene

"Is this a private fight, or can anyone join?"
– Olde Irish saying

Now that you have a better understanding of the role of non-verbal communication and delivery style in intervention, we can take a closer look at what to say, when to say it, and how to say it. Having pre-practiced phrases in mind will help you know what to say at the point of impact. Engagement phrases, redirections, and persuasion are three word-based tools that will help you, even during the most stressful of situations.

Engagement Phrases

Engagement phrases are phrases you can use to quickly intervene, get someone's attention, or divert a conversation. Effective engagement phrases need to be short (remember the economy of words) and long enough to tactfully get your point across without escalating the situation.

In order for an engagement phrase to be effective, you have to ensure that your word choice and delivery style match your intended message. This will ensure that the engagement phrase is delivered in a way that is non-accusatory and non-judgmental. A slight alteration in your word choice alone can create a different impression and have a much different impact.

For example:

- Instead of saying, "*Stop yelling,*" try saying: "*Take a deep breath and then tell me what happened.*"

- Instead of saying, "*Be quiet,*" or "*Shut up,*" try saying: "*Could you please use a softer voice?*"

- Instead of saying, "*What's wrong with you?*" try saying: "*What did I miss that has you feeling this way?*"

Here are additional examples of common engagement phrases:

1. "This is *ABC Organization*. That is not what we are about."
2. "You may not have offended me, but your words/actions/ behaviors may have offended someone else."
3. "I understand that you have every right to feel angry, but it is not okay for you to threaten me or others."
4. "Could you please clarify what you just said? I'm not sure I understood that correctly."
5. "Do you really feel that way about 'x' person/group/ behavior?
6. "I didn't expect that from you."
7. "Really?"
8. "You have always done a good job, and I appreciate that."
9. "We've always been able to work things out in the past."
10. "Could you please find a respectful way to ask/say that?"
11. "I understand you're upset; I hear you. I'm here now, and I want to help."
12. "I'm here to help, and if I can't help you, I will find you someone who can. Okay?"

13. How can I help/how can we fix this if you keep yelling at me?"

14. "Could you please explain to me what is going on from your perspective/as you see it?"

15. "Right now, this is a small issue; let's work together so it doesn't become 'x.'"

16. "That didn't necessarily offend me, but it may have offended someone else."

17. "Hey now, take it back. You didn't really mean that, did you?"

18. "Could you please choose/use another word?"

19. "Hey, we're friends, right? Could we please talk about ..."

20. "Let's think about that for a second."

There are a few other things to keep in mind when delivering engagement phrases:

- Avoid using words like "sir" or "ma'am" to eliminate the tension and avoid the awkwardness of misidentifying someone or setting off gender triggers.

- Remember the precision of word choice. Make sure you say what you mean and mean what you say. Words mean different things to different people.

- Consider using the phrases in combination, as part of a redirection, or to build context as part of the persuasion sequence.

- Empathize with their feelings, not their inappropriate behaviors.

Redirection

Redirection is a method taught in the Vistelar *Non-Escalation, De-Escalation, and Crisis Management* training program used to de-escalate verbal resistance (such as shouting, ranting, or refusal) or a verbal assault (insults or direct verbal attacks) in a way that allows you to bring the conversation back to the issue at hand. The goal of using a redirection is to prevent a verbal confrontation from escalating further. Here is an example:

Acknowledge the comment → Back to the issue

With this redirection, you acknowledge the other person's comments with a statement like, *"I can appreciate that," "I hear you," "I got that,"* or *"I see,"* and then structure your next statement(s) to get back to the issue at hand.

Here are a few examples:

- *"I hear you; however, we have an issue to address. Can you work with me here?"*

- *"I appreciate that you have had problems in the past. However, you haven't worked with me before. Let's see what I can do to help."*

- *"Is there something I did to make you angry? I apologize if I did something wrong, but can you please not swear at me so we can resolve this?"*

In using the redirection method, do not concern yourself with the other person's abusive comments or dismissal. Your job is not to fix their attitude; it is to change their behavior.

In looking at the application of engagement phrases and redirections, let's revisit a few of the common excuses for inappropriate behavior mentioned earlier:

Excuses	In the Moment Responses
"That's just the way they talk. They didn't mean anything by it."	*"They may not have offended me, but that may have offended someone else. Their intent isn't the issue; it's the impact."*
"It's nothing. Ignore it."	*"Well, I found it offensive, and others may have too."*
"We all face it; toughen up."	*"Just because we all face it doesn't make it right. I don't see how that comment creates a supportive atmosphere."*
"I'd stay quiet if I were you. She is our star performer."	*"So are we putting performance metrics above our company values now? Because we value treating all people with dignity and respect, and those actions are not respectful."*
"It's always been that way. No supervisor will do anything about it."	*"Really? I've worked with Chris as a supervisor for a long time and know him to follow through on what he says he's going to do."*

Persuasion

Persuasion is another method taught in the Vistelar *Non-Escalation, De-Escalation, and Crisis Management* training program used to achieve cooperation, collaboration, or consensus while avoiding escalation to a verbal or physical confrontation.

Persuasion works best when you:

1. Are respectful.
2. Provide solid reasoning.
3. Appeal to their emotions.

Being respectful is accomplished by starting every interaction with a universal greeting, and listening rather than talking. Since people are more likely to agree or cooperate with people they like, trust, and view as credible, being respectful is the most powerful contributor to persuasion. You should not begin persuasion until you have introduced yourself with a universal greeting and listened to their answer to the relevant question (Step 4 directly below):

To use the universal greeting:

1. Use a (neutral) appropriate greeting (such as "hello").
2. State your name and affiliation (who you work for and your role).
3. State the reason for the contact (explain why you are talking with them).
4. Ask the relevant question (explain why you are speaking with them).

Here is an example of what this sounds like in action:

"Hello. My name is Heyden, and I'm the manager here. I overheard you swearing quite loudly in the lobby on your phone call. Could you please keep your voice down and choose more respectful language?"

(Please note that this is just one application example of the universal greeting. The relevant question does not have to be a compliance-related question, but in this particular case, it is.)

If the person you have approached does not cooperate, verbally resists, or insults you, then you would proceed to using persuasion. The three-step persuasion sequence provides an opportunity to appeal to their logic and emotions, and it works like this:

1. Explain why, then confirm their understanding.

To prevent people from imagining their own reasons as to why you are asking them to do something:

- State the reason for your request (usually due to a law, policy, rule or prior agreement),

- Explain the rationale for the reason, and

- Then ask if they understand the explanation.

Using the example from above, it would sound like this:

"Our policy is to create and maintain an emotionally and physically safe environment for everyone, and loud shouting and swearing goes against that policy because it frightens people. Does that make sense to you?"

If the person pushes back, refuses, or delivers a personal or organizational insult, proceed to the next step.

2. **Offer options, and let them choose.** Start by offering them a positive option. Make sure you sound positive and upbeat, almost as if you are advocating for them and this choice. Then follow up by offering a less desirable option, and make sure you deliver it in a way that it doesn't sound like a threat. Then, empower them to decide.

    Using the example from above, it would sound like this:

    "I understand that you are frustrated. However, we have some good options here. It's a beautiful day out, and there's an outdoor public waiting area just outside that door. You're more than welcome to go enjoy some sun and make that phone call outside. However, if you're unwilling to step outside to that courtyard, and you're unwilling to stop shouting and swearing, I will have to ask you to leave the premises. Given that you drove a long way to get here, I'm sure there's a good reason for your visit, and I know your time is valuable to you. Are you willing to work with me here and just finish that phone call outside in the courtyard?"

If the person continues to push back, refuses, or delivers a personal or organizational insult, proceed to the next step.

3. **Finally, give them the opportunity to reconsider.** Give them a chance to save face while reminding them why cooperation is the best course of action.

Here is an example of what this sounds like in action:

"I understand your frustration, and if I were in your position, I might be too. I know you just want to vent, and I'd love for you to be able to do that – outside – and in private. Is there anything I can say to get you to change your mind?"

If the other person has not cooperated after this third step, your options will vary depending on the situation, and it is important that you know what the next course of action is. In this case, it may be the need to call security, or perhaps a different staff member could come and try and talk to the individual.

What if Word-Based Methods Fail?

Non-escalation and de-escalation are about employing different strategies toward a desired result: reducing intensity, conflict, or a potentially violent situation. However, de-escalation must be understood as a process, not a particular outcome, and even if you do everything "right," word-based methods alone may not be enough to resolve the situation.

Despite our best efforts:

- The persuasion sequence can end without cooperation (as explained in the example above), or

- A clearly articulable safety concern could justify taking some other action (such as the person increasing aggression or displaying at-risk or harmful behavior to themselves or others).

When either of these criteria is met, you must take appropriate action, which includes these two steps:

- Know your options for taking action (which will vary depending on your role in the organization), and

- Have a pre-planned response to situations you will likely face (by using when-then/thinking scenarios).

If you identify safety risks, notice pre-incident indicators, are exposed to gateway behaviors, or if word-based methods fail, your best option might not be to engage but to leave, to call a supervisor, or worst-case scenario, possibly security or 911. If you believe some form of physical engagement could occur, leave via a predetermined escape route.

After Action Considerations: Closure, Debrief, and Documentation

If you were or are involved in any form of incident, there are several after-action considerations to keep in mind, including incident closure, debriefing, and documentation.

First of all, Closure is a method taught in the Vistelar *Non-Escalation, De-Escalation, and Crisis Management* training program for ending all interactions safely and on a positive note, regardless of how negative the event may have been. It also helps build a better foundation for any possible future interactions.

Here are a few reminders related to closure

- Practice empathy: Gather information; act based on how you would feel if you were in the exact same situation; show respect and demonstrate concern. Consider giving a post-incident Universal Greeting and reintroduce yourself now that emotions have settled.

- Respond, don't react: Maintain emotional equilibrium, and pay attention to proxemics, non-verbals, verbals, and para-verbals.

- Exhaust all reasonable attempts to resolve refusals: De-escalate resistance, manage crisis, and ensure everyone is safe.

- Acknowledge that things may not have gone as either of you would have liked and state that you are hopeful for a more positive interaction in the future.

Secondly, you need to debrief the incident with others. This could include anyone who witnessed the event, assisted with the intervention, managers, or any other personnel associated with the after-action review process.

Debriefs are highly valuable because they:

- Help those involved decompress and can reduce the possibility of psychological harm by talking about what has happened.

- Set the tone for learning and improved team response.

- Create space where facts can be reviewed and misconceptions about the incident can be corrected.

- Focus on what was learned from the incident that should be used (or avoided) in the future.

- Help streamline internal and external processes or policies.

Additionally, in the event of a serious incident, such as a physical assault or the need for physical intervention, a formal (or administrative) post-incident review will likely evaluate the reasonableness of the actions taken and will be evaluated in relation to:

1. The totality of the circumstances,
2. Your training and experience (the perspective of a reasonable person in a similar position),
3. Who was on the scene,
4. At the moment the decision was made,

5. Without 20/20 hindsight, and

6. In circumstances that are often tense, uncertain, and rapidly evolving.

These six elements are critical in assessing actions taken during an incident and are directly from the 1989 U.S. Supreme Court decision (Graham v. Connor).

Additionally, your actions may be evaluated in relation to the nature or severity of the offense, if the person displayed active resistance, or if their actions posed an immediate threat to you or someone else. These are known as the Graham Factors, and for this reason, you will need to show both proper and legal decision-making and the proper articulation of the event. This means you will have to be able to explain why you did what you did when you were within policy and the law to do so. "Reasonable action" for some may seem quite different to someone facing an aggressor in the moment than to someone just analyzing the situation after the fact and at their leisure (this point was flushed out in the 1992 Circuit Court decision (Smith v. Freland 1992).

Finally, if you were or are involved in any form of a reportable incident, file a report according to your organization's policies and procedures. This will be covered more in-depth later in the book.

Such reports will typically include a description of the incident, your attempt to manage it, and the outcomes of the incident.

In deciding what to report, consider a reportable lateral violence incident as any attempt to emotionally, socially, or economically harm another.

It's important to note that incidents of lateral violence are often underreported for a variety of reasons, including:

• There is not a consistent organizational definition of violence.

- There is a pervasive acceptance of threatening behavior and violence as part of the job.

- There is a belief that a threat of violence is not significant enough to report.

- Employees may be embarrassed and hesitant to report violent behavior.

- Employees may feel they don't have the time to write a report.

- Employees may fear accusations of incompetence or think their employer might assume they were the cause of the violence.

- There is a lack of supervisor support.

While avenues for reporting are organization-specific, the importance of reporting cannot be understated. In order for a problem to be addressed, people must be aware of its existence. It is critical to have records in place that will help the employer understand the extent of the problem(s), investigate them, and take actions to stop the behaviors from happening again in the future.

Work with your human resources personnel to ensure that your organization has a confidential and centralized reporting system in place with anonymous reporting options. Reference the Vistelar Workplace Violence Prevention and Intervention training program for more information (please refer to the section titled "Who is Vistelar" at the end of the book).

Key Takeaways

- Bystander intervention moments are less often about what to "do" and are more often about what to "say" and when to say it.
- Consider and apply these foundational elements of delivery style:
  - To whom you say it (your audience).
  - What you say (the content, your word choice).
  - When you say it (timing).
  - Where you say it (the location).
  - Why you say it (by presenting your evidence, reasoning, desired outcome).
  - How you say it (your pace, pitch, tone, inflection).
  - How you look (non-verbal communication).
- Beyond delivery, using precise language matters during an intervention.
  - Engagement phrases are non-judgmental and non-escalatory phrases that can get someone's attention or divert a conversation.
  - Redirection is a quick and effective method of turning a conversation back towards a professional goal.
  - Persuasion is a de-escalation method for gaining cooperation or collaboration.
- If you are involved in any form of incident, there are several after-action considerations to keep in mind:
  - Closure is a method of ending interactions safely and on a positive note and sets the foundation for future interactions.
  - Debriefing is important for reducing the possibility of psychological harm by talking about what has happened.
  - Appropriate and thorough documentation helps the employer understand the extent of the problem(s), investigate them, and take actions to stop the behaviors from happening again in the future.

Jill Weisensel

CHAPTER EIGHT
Active Threat Prevention and Preparedness

You can make a difference. Violence and threats of violence often result from frustration and a communication breakdown. People want to be heard and understood; empower them to speak up. Then listen—truly listen—to identify the signposts along the way and stay "left of bang."

As cited throughout this book, lateral violence can lead to physical violence, and in the workplace, lateral violence can kill. In a study referenced in the book The Price of Incivility, Drs. Christine Porath and Christine Pearson found that a shocking 94% of victims claim they somehow settle their scores with the offenders. In addition, if you recall from Chapter One, there is a direct correlation between workplace lateral violence and active shooter incidents. (Modell, 2013)

The dissociation of those victimized and the subsequent desire for retaliation could result in an active threat incident. (Morrison, Lindo, Aiken, & Chin, 2017) An active threat is defined as any incident that, by its deliberate nature, creates an immediate threat or presents an imminent danger.

Therefore, even though the focus of this book is on lateral violence, it would be an inappropriate omission not to include information relevant to the prevention and preparation for an active threat incident.

Active threat incidents have sadly become a common occurrence. If you conduct an online search of active shooter events, the return will be countless pages of results referencing dozens of incidents. The three most well-known active shooter events involved schools: Columbine High School (1999), Virginia Tech (2007), and the Sandy Hook Elementary school shooting (2012). However, only a third of active shooter events happen in schools, while the majority happen in other "soft-target" environments such as workplaces, places of worship, and retail environments.

Active threat prevention includes following your organization's workplace violence policies and procedures, which may include any or all of the following:

- Workplace violence zero tolerance.

- Eliminating gateway behaviors (e.g., shouting, cursing, name-calling, aggressive posturing), and if they occur, responding appropriately.

- Mandatory reporting of pre-incident indicators, overt threats, and workplace violence incidents, with impunity and anonymity, if desired.

- Mandatory training in threat assessment and safety measures.

- Mandatory reporting to the authorities.

Active threat incident prevention also involves many additional strategies, methods, and tactics, including:

- Identifying pre-incident indicators.

- Establishing situational awareness.

- Being cognizant of violence triggers.

- Applying both non-escalation and de-escalation methods

- Knowing your options and having a pre-planned, practiced response for taking appropriate action.

If you experience violations of your workplace violence policies and procedures, document and report them. Policies and procedures are of no value if they are not practiced.

With respect to active shooter incidents, there are several identifiable behaviors (or red flag pre-incident indicators) you should be watching for. While not always predictive of violent behavior, specific, identifiable behaviors of concern include:

- Past behavior.

- Often exhibiting angry or argumentative behavior.

- Blaming others for their problems.

- Failing to take responsibility for their own actions.

- Retaliating against perceived injustice.

- Increasing belligerence.

- Ominous, specific threats.

- Hypersensitivity to criticism.

- Recent acquisition of or fascination with weapons.

- Preoccupation with violent themes.

- Interest in recently publicized violent events.

- Outbursts of anger.

- Extreme disorganization.

- Noticeable changes in behavior.

- Homicidal or suicidal comments or threats.

No one specific behavior determines that someone will engage in active killing, but a cluster of several may. It is important to understand these warning signs and their role in leading up to an active shooter or other potentially violent event.

In addition to increasing situational awareness and identifying red flags, organizations can work to reduce and prevent violent incidents through target hardening and environmental design.

A few of the common target hardening concepts are:

- Reinforcing current policies and procedures.

- Improving access control, such as limiting entry and exit points and clearly identifying building and property boundaries.

- Displaying visible signs and safety rules identifying open and closed access areas.

- Monitoring and ensuring lockable doors are locked throughout the workday.

- Managing the flow of pedestrian traffic within the organization.

- Defining and enforcing a visitor screening process upon entry.

- Enforcing visible ID systems, such as lanyards, key cards, or name tags with a photo of the person wearing the badge.

- Using monitored surveillance, such as camera systems or security personnel.

- Improving lighting.

- Identifying blind spots throughout the facility that hinder surveillance cameras.

- Visibly enforcing and reinforcing on-site security.

Your organization should have policies and procedures on active threats and implement a training program. Part of that training program should include an active threat preparedness plan, sometimes called an Emergency Action Plan, or EAP. A well-thought-out plan is important because each active threat situation is unique, and active threat events unfold and escalate rapidly. Furthermore, every facility is unique in building structure and design, the number of employees within, variability in public access, and day-to-day activities.

Before an effective active threat response plan can be put into place, conduct a review of the current location, building structure, and staff schedules. This review should include an organizational questionnaire and a complete site assessment.

An active threat preparedness plan should include (at a minimum):

1. The definition of an active threat.
2. Immediate action steps for defense.
3. An emergency communication plan.
4. Event priority actions, such as escape, barricade, and defend.
5. What to expect from law enforcement on scene.
6. What to expect or what can be done by employees during the event.
7. The identification of assembly or staging areas.
8. After action considerations.

All of these steps need to be flushed out and understood. This cannot just be a document placed into a file; each element should be trained.

Training will better prepare individuals in the event an active threat occurs. Determine the appropriate frequency, length, and delivery format for your organization. Common delivery formats for active threat preparedness include:

- Videos or audio.
- Online learning modules.
- Open question and answer forums.

- Lecture or guest speakers (such as local law enforcement) on the topic.

- Hands-on skill-building activities.

- Round table or "tabletop" exercises.

- Live scenario or simulation exercises.

Creating an effective active threat preparedness plan requires three critical steps:

1. **Planning out potential timelines.**

   An initial timeline should map an effective hiring and termination processes long before an active shooter event could unfold. This includes but is not limited to employee evaluations, performance improvement plans, and early warning systems. Additionally, identifying a timeline can include the first moment the intruder(s) or attacker(s) would enter the property all the way through the time it will take for you or the police to arrive and stop the threat.

2. **Ensuring everyone understands the various roles and responsibilities in the event of an active threat incident.**

   You should train and dedicate staff to help in the event of an emergency or evacuation. These staff may play the following parts in incident intervention and response:

   - Help defuse violent situations while acting within legal and ethical guidelines.

   - Prevent, disrupt, and deter crime.

   - Minimize property loss and damage.

   - Provide technical advice and support regarding physical security.

- Promote an ongoing security awareness program.

- Assist with conducting investigations of threats or incidents of violence.

- Act as a liaison with local authorities.

- Requesting arrests for acts of violence, if provided with this authority.

- Prepare for the prosecution of arrested individuals.

- Assist in the evacuation of people with varying emotional and physical capabilities.

3. **Creating plan sustainability.**

Additionally, this plan is only useful if it is visible, well understood by all in your organization, and constantly in front of them. This topic needs more than a "one-and-done" rollout. You can ensure the thoroughness, relevancy, and sustainability of your active threat preparedness plan by:

- Investing in training or instructors.

- Reading articles.

- Listening to podcasts and webinars.

- Attending conferences on best practices.

- Reviewing video of incidents with debriefs.

- Engaging in daily huddles or roll calls.

- Holding weekly briefings, monthly shift training, quarterly section drills, and/or bi-annual organizational exercises.

For additional information on this topic refer to the Vistelar *Active Shooter Preparedness and Response* training program (please reference the section titled "Who is Vistelar" at the end of the book).

Key Takeaways

1. An active threat is any incident that creates an immediate threat or presents an imminent danger.
2. Active threat prevention requires following your organization's workplace violence policies and procedures. Additional threat prevention strategies, methods, and tactics include:
    - Identifying pre-incident indicators.
    - Establishing situational awareness.
    - Being cognizant of violence triggers.
    - Non-escalation methods.
    - De-escalation methods.
    - Knowing your options and having a pre-planned, practiced response for taking appropriate action.
3. An effective active threat preparedness plan requires three critical steps:
    - Planning out potential timelines.
    - Ensuring everyone knows roles and responsibilities in the event of an active threat incident.
    - Creating plan sustainability.

PART TWO CONCLUSION

Throughout part two of this book I explained the importance of creating an ethical and professional presence, and emphasized the need for professional and ethical intervention. I outlined numerous strategies for improving situational awareness, resiliency, and identifying situations that may require some form of intervention – recognizing the ways in which we can be part of the solution and not a part of the problem.

The TAKES ACTION acronym alone provides the framework necessary for knowing how and when to intervene. Mastering proxemic management, risk and threat assessment, communication alignment, and the use of engagement phrases will equip you for success in managing these situations in your workplace. Remember that intervention moments, those moments that will either build or destroy trust amongst your co-workers and friends, are less often about what to "do" and are more often about what to "say" and when to say it.

You will never know when your heads-up awareness, empathy, and kind words could be exactly what someone needed to prevent them from making a short-term decision having devastating long-term results.

PART THREE
Best Practices and Next Steps for Taking Action

···

CHAPTER NINE
Human Resources: Best Practice Policy Considerations

Throughout this book, we have explained the importance and value of maintaining an environment that is incompatible with emotional and physical violence, accomplished by creating and maintaining an organizational culture that won't allow it. It is your organizational culture that will drive behaviors, and those behaviors will drive outcomes.

However, even the healthiest cultures should be supported by robust workplace violence prevention programs and policies. Additionally, OSHA recommends that employers establish and maintain a violence prevention plan as part of their safety and health programs.

The following section offers best practices and a starting point for developing your own workplace violence program.

Preliminary Considerations for Organizational Leadership

Before developing your violence prevention program and associated policies, there are several preliminary questions for organizational leadership to consider, and they are categorized below.

Related to Accountability and Support

- Have you conducted a comprehensive gap analysis (to assess the current state versus the desired future state) of any workplace violence prevention efforts or policies, including an assessment of organizational culture and readiness?

- Have you conducted a safety and security assessment of the physical work environment to identify the physical and psychosocial hazards that may increase the likelihood of violence occurring?

- Does your program have a system of accountability for all involved managers and employees?

- Will management support the (new) policy? Your policies are only as good as your ability to follow them.

- Do you have the appropriate funding and resource allocation to support and implement the program/policy?

- Do you have a post-incident response plan in place that includes investigative practices that will defend you in the event of litigation? Does the post-incident response plan include comprehensive counseling or support options for those who have experienced or witnessed incidents of lateral violence?

- Have you determined what type of insurance would need to be in place for specific events, such as a terrorist act versus an armed assailant? Worker's compensation only covers injured workers. Do you have property coverage that includes business interruption and loss of physical property?

Related to Community Readiness and the Prioritization of Workplace Violence Prevention

- Does your organization prioritize workplace safety and the reduction of psychosocial hazards to create an emotionally and physically safe work environment?

- Does your organization have an equal commitment to worker safety and the emotional/physical health and wellness of patients/clients/customers?

- Does your workplace have a plan in place for identifying incidents that may be precursors to physical violence?

- Does your workplace have a plan in place for identifying high-risk terminations?

Related to the Reporting of Incidents

- Does your current work environment encourage people to come forward with information?

- Do your reporting policies include no reprisals or retaliation for reporting?

- Have you established a consistent reporting protocol? Identify multiple avenues in reporting to ensure that threats or violent acts are dealt with in a timely manner. Consider the use of reporting hotlines.

- Have you broadly communicated the reporting protocol you implemented? The more your employees are aware of the channels of reporting, the more likely they are to report information.

- Have you implemented and enforced a violence response policy? Have you determined which employees need to be involved in responding to incidents and trained them? Clearly outline and put in place disciplinary measures for those who fail to report, fail to respond, or engage in workplace violence. This includes written warnings, progressive discipline, demotion, days off, and, potentially, termination.

Related to Hiring Practices

- Are careful hiring practices (and background checks) in place? A background screening will prevent hiring individuals presenting a risk of workplace violence. The best predictor of future violence is past violent behavior. Consider working with a background check provider to help you identify employees who best fit your hiring requirements.

When drafting policies, also consider:

- Establishing a Conflict Prevention Social Contract and including language in the policy that supports and reinforces it.

- Drafting comprehensive policies that prohibit physical, verbal, and all forms of lateral violence and include disciplinary consequences up to termination.

- Training your managers, supervisors, and staff to take appropriate action and intervene when it is safe to do so.

- Training everyone to take responsibility and be the "eyes and ears."

It is not enough to adopt the "see something, say something" mentality. You must train them on what to look for and what to do. These are the foundational elements of being alert and decisive. Additionally, we must understand that if you "see something" and don't "say something," we have to recognize that we have become complicit.

In Chapter 7, we touched on after-action considerations. Your post-incident response should be formalized and predictable. It will allow you to assess all of the processes and people that were impacted and diagnose root problems so you can create an action plan for preventing it from happening again in the future.

Your after-action considerations should include:

- Comprehensive documentation of the incident that includes who, what, where, when, and how. If applicable, collect statements from those involved.

- Closure (for yourself and everyone involved) to end interactions safely and on a positive note for future interactions.

- Debriefing (to assist in after-action closure and improving future performance).

- Appropriate documentation through your organization's avenues of reporting (so that your organization can take appropriate action)

- Ongoing support for all staff (such as EAP support, the availability of on-site counselors, and follow-up or follow-through from supervision).

Finally, your violence prevention program should also:

- Be available to all employees, including managers and supervisors; all employees should receive specific training concerning its content and implementation.

- Reflect the level and nature of threats faced by employees.

- Include a worksite analysis to find existing or potential hazards for lateral violence (evaluate credible threats, evaluate capabilities, identify vulnerabilities, and assess the consequences).

- Include metrics for measuring the effectiveness of your violence prevention program, such as:

- Tracking employees' progress in reducing work-related assaults.

- A reduction in the severity of injuries sustained by employees.

- The number of threats to worker safety.

Key Takeaways

- Best practices when developing a workplace violence prevention program include:
  - Conducting thorough background checks.
  - Establishing a consistent reporting protocol.
  - Implementing and enforcing a violence response policy.
  - Training all employees in what to look for, what to do, and what to expect when they report.
- Lateral violence prevention policies should consider:
  - The emotional and physical health of all employees.
  - Appropriate allocation of authority and resources.
  - A safety and security assessment of the physical work environment to identify the physical and psychological hazards that may increase the likelihood of violence occurring.
  - Establishing a conflict prevention social contract.

CHAPTER TEN

Conclusion: Now That We Know ... Now What?

Throughout this book, you have learned that everyone plays a crucial role in creating a safe workplace—one that you can be proud to be a part of and in which you feel physically and emotionally safer. I sincerely hope you enjoyed this book, but more importantly, I hope you have learned some of the strategies and skills necessary to end lateral violence.

Whether you have perpetrated, condoned, ignored, or been victimized, you can make a difference.

"What we do today, right now, will have an accumulated effect on all of our tomorrows."

– Alexandra Stoddard, philosopher and bestselling author of 28 books

Studies have shown that those who engage in lateral violence remember doing so. In one nursing study alone, upwards of 85.5% of participant nurses reported feeling "deeply sorry" for their actions. (Ayakdas & Arslantas, 2018)

With that being said, what can you do? What are some things to consider if you have found yourself engaging in these behaviors, perhaps because it's all you've ever known? Even if you didn't mean

159

any harm, or if you weren't aware that you engaged in behaviors that are harmful to others, it is probable that if you've made it to this part of the book, you've realized the damage caused by incivility and you're willing to take ownership in improving.

Being aware of the behavior is the first step. Perhaps it has gotten back to you that other employees have complained about your behavior, comments you've made in meetings, facial expressions, or your attitude towards a particular person or topic. This alone serves as a data point and one to deeply reflect on.

Wait. What?

Yes, reflect on the feedback you're getting. Seek out additional feedback from a trusted colleague, personal coach, or mentor. Seek out additional feedback and perspectives from 360 surveys, and don't get defensive. Instead of shutting it down and dismissing the input from others, ask yourself, "How have I been acting that could have made them feel this way?" Ask, "What has happened to them?" Ask yourself these questions rather than assuming something is clearly "wrong with them." You'll never look good trying to make someone else look bad. Full stop.

Also, look inward to evaluate your behavior. Yes, self-work and internal work are hard. It is highly uncomfortable. So it will take both vulnerability and courage to move from behaving uncivilly to civilly. Identify the behaviors you want to change and write them down. Perhaps journal or keep a reminder card that lists the action you want to change and what to do about it. Then, make a conscious effort to do those things. This could be as simple as remembering to smile at work or using words like "please" and "thank you." It could be as simple as being sincere in your gratitude or making a greater effort to listen.

Dedicated effort and small changes will lead to big results in behavior change.

"All this will not be finished in the first 100 days. Nor will it be finished in the first 1,000 days. Nor even perhaps in our lifetime on this planet. But let us begin."

– John F. Kennedy

And what if you've now realized that you've been the target of these behaviors and that it is unacceptable?

First, do not fall into the trap of assuming that lateral violence is the same as schoolyard bullying. There are decades of research showing that "fighting back" (as you would, perhaps, on a schoolyard playground) is not effective. Researchers Christine Pearson and Christine Porath put it this way in their 2009 book, *The Cost of Bad Behavior*:

Workplace offenders have very little in common with schoolyard bullies. Two-thirds of workplace offenders have the power of the organizational hierarchy behind them; they call the shots on the corporate playing field. Although some high-power organizational offenders may seem at first to accept your pushback, you must not forget that they have resources, connections, and hierarchical perspectives that exceed your own. That would mean, in the playground analogy, that the principal and the teachers would be the bullies.

Do not sit idly by. Throughout the book, I've cited numerous reasons why long-term exposure to these behaviors is dangerous for your health, including that those exposed to lateral violence and workplace incivility over time are 35-55% more likely to be diagnosed with a major disease—such as cardiac problems, stroke, and diabetes—than those who have not been exposed. (Sull & Sull, 2022) Remember, doing nothing is never a neutral option.

So what *can* you do?

In addition to all of the low-level and point-of-impact intervention options presented in this book, I can offer a few more recommendations through my own observations, experiences, and collective understanding of both the research and best practices.

Resilience in the Face of Victimization

The first step is recognizing that you've been the target of this behavior, and it is going to take its toll on you. Regardless of how resilient you are and how "strong" you are, this type of behavior will impact you emotionally and physically. Surround yourself with a network of people who will support you and provide you with guidance you trust.

Then you have a decision to make, and that decision will depend completely on your specific circumstances and your level of comfort with the situation:

- You can try to minimize the amount of time you're exposed to the offender.

- You can try to vary the types of interactions you have with the offender.

- You can try to work through the situation by speaking with the offender directly.

- You can choose to work through the situation by speaking with allies and creating your own internal support network.

- You can speak to someone of higher authority.

There are many pros and cons and variables in each of these scenarios. For some people, minimizing the amount of time you're exposed to the offender may be impossible, such as when this person is your direct supervisor. In this case, varying the types of interactions may be a possibility, such as communicating more via email or phone rather than face-to-face. Or, maybe you can coordinate that another supervisor is in the room whenever you need to have a critical conversation with that person.

Speaking with an ally is helpful when you have someone who

knows both you and the offender. It is possible this person "has the ear" of the offender, in which case, the offender may be more open to suggestions from that person or more receptive to change.

Speaking to a person in authority is an option that requires trust and tact, but it can be done effectively. Remember to relay objective information—the facts of the situation. Focus on articulating the offender's behaviors and how they make you feel. Describe how they are impacting your ability to most effectively do your job. Resist the urge to make it personal; this conversation should not be a bashing session describing all the reasons why you "don't like" the person. If you are hesitant to have a conversation like this alone, consider bringing an ally, perhaps a co-worker who has witnessed the behavior and can help you relay what is happening while also being less emotionally invested. If the thought of having this conversation is intimidating for you, consider writing down your thoughts and key points on paper and have it with you when you start the conversation.

Finally, you can also reframe your thinking and change your approach to the situation. If the relationship between you and this person has become that of an immovable object meets an unstoppable force, resist the urge to distill your options down to a despondent "it's either them or me, one of us will have to go" mentality. I've been in this situation and endured it for over nine years. I thought the end would never be in sight. It was suffocating. It was impossible to focus at work. It was impossible to sleep or eat.

At times, it had gotten so bad that I was certain I would have to trade in all that I had worked for just so I could survive. But then, one day, I realized the behaviors wouldn't change, and I could do little more than address them as they came up, in front of peers. Soon other employees took notice and started standing up, calling out the behaviors and offering suggestions for improvement. Slowly, over time, things got a *little* better. Not great. But better. And then I realized

I had made the decision to "take the high road." Not the decision to "turn the other cheek" and ignore it, but to act at a higher moral and ethical level than that person was professionally able to.

Pearson and Porath (2006) note that people targeted by incivility have various rationales for reframing their thinking rather than seeking retribution. Some of these reasons are:

- Citing "cosmic justice," the belief that people like that will eventually "do themselves in."

- Feeling apathy toward the offender, thinking the person is not worth their "time" or "effort."

- Viewing it as a job requirement, that they have to "work with the person" and they will continue to do their job, but perhaps not alone with that person.

- Believing that it's bad timing, that they'll take action eventually, but not now.

Finally, in organizations in which toxic corporate culture is well established and has free rein, reframing your thinking may also involve "withdrawing emotionally from your job." (Pearson & Porath, 2006)

I cannot make this point better than Stanford Professor Dr. Robert Sutton. In his 2007 book *The No Asshole Rule*, he states:

All this talk about passion, commitment, and identification within an organization is absolutely correct if you are in a good job and are treated with dignity and respect. But it is hypocritical nonsense to the millions of people who are trapped in jobs and companies where they feel oppressed and humiliated ...

If you've tried the options described above and nothing is improving the situation, perhaps look to see if a lateral transfer position is open and available before making a decision to quit.

Ultimately, your health and personal happiness are far more important than your organization's bottom line.

"Leaders lead from the front. The most powerful leadership tool you have is your own personal example."
— John Wooden, legendary American basketball coach

And finally, if you have the privilege of being an organizational leader, please do not underestimate the influence, power, and responsibility you have in creating systemic organizational change. Truly, you are in the best position to have an impact during every touchpoint of the organizational change process: from the planning and preparation - all the way through the implementation, management, and maintenance of change.

Ultimately, your health and personal happiness are far more important than your organization's bottom line.

I would be hard-pressed to identify a more rewarding experience or accomplishment for a transformational leader than being able to state that you were on the front line of true organizational change—a change that reduced workplace toxicity, improved organizational culture and productivity, and one that will help your employees not only survive, but thrive.

"We carry with us, as human beings, not just the capacity to be kind but the very choice of kindness. You see, the way we react to a situation is a true test of character. Never forget that."
— Brent Lindeque, motivational speaker and change agent

Key Takeaways

- Whether you have perpetrated, condoned, ignored, or fallen victim to lateral violence, you have a crucial role to play in creating an emotionally, psychologically, and physically safe workplace environment.

- Self-reflect and ensure that you are not part of the problem. And if you are, make a commitment to change your behavior.

- If you have been the target of lateral violence, do not sit idly by. Seek out an ally, solicit feedback, and determine the best course of action depending on your specific circumstances.

- If you are an organizational leader and in a position of authority, take action to create organizational change.

Afterword

Ending Lateral Violence

The goal of this book is to provide you with the knowledge, skills, and abilities to:

- Prevent workplace violence via the practice of "non-escalation."

- Recognize and correct gateway behaviors and other conditions that lead to workplace violence.

- Identify pre-incident indicators that can be a precursor to violence.

- De-escalate and recover from situations that could lead to violence at the point of development.

- Act appropriately when faced with violence.

Depending on your role within your organization, you may find this information sufficient to be the first line of defense against workplace violence by:

- Being situationally aware.

- Applying the non-escalation and de-escalation methods to your interactions.

- Taking the appropriate action when word-based methods fail.

The Impact of Addressing Lateral Violence and Training Intervention Skills

Sharing this information across and at all levels of your organization will increase understanding of lateral violence and what to do in the presence of it.

The most obvious benefits of sharing this information are increased awareness, personal safety, reduced risk and liability, and fewer worker's compensation claims.

Additional benefits include employee retention, improved performance, and improved service delivery and recovery. However, the bottom line is that taking a proactive approach to addressing lateral violence results in a cultural transformation that will improve everyone's experience.

In terms of employee performance, the National Business Research Institute lists five key factors that affect productivity:

- Nature of relationship with supervisor.

- Level of morale and motivation.

- Level of job enjoyment.

- Health and well-being.

- Effectiveness of technology use.

In other words, employee performance is largely driven by the quality of interpersonal relations, which is driven by the skills discussed throughout this book:

- Verbal and paraverbal communication: What we say and how we say it.

- Non-verbal communication: The message we communicate without words.

- Listening skills: How we interpret both the verbal and non-verbal messages sent by others.

- Negotiation: Working with others to find a mutually agreeable outcome.

- Problem-solving: Working with others to identify, define, and solve problems.

- Decision making: Exploring and analyzing options to make sound decisions.

- Assertiveness: Freely communicating our values, ideas, beliefs, opinions, needs, and wants.

Deficiencies in these skills (poor communication, inadequate listening, bad negotiations, subpar problem solving, coercive actions, and poor decision making) contribute to conflict.

Even the final skill on the list—assertiveness—is related to how we manage conflict. Most people within organizations struggle with conflict, and rather than being assertive, they avoid conflict, appease people by giving in, or become an aggressor towards another person.

When people avoid conflict or give in rather than deal with conflict directly, negative things happen and have repercussions that reverberate throughout the entire organization. If conflicts go unresolved, resentment builds, and frustration grows. Ignored inappropriate behaviors get positively reinforced, and the undercurrent of organizational conflict can escalate to emotional or physical violence. The key to breaking this cycle is understanding that no matter who you are, you have an important role in ending lateral violence:

- Those who have perpetrated can commit to behavior change.

- Those who have been victimized are supported and can speak up.

- Those who have witnessed incidents can intervene.

- And those who are leaders can influence others and initiate change.

"I believe that one of the most important things to learn in life is that you can make a difference in your community no matter who you are or where you live. I have seen so many good deeds, people helped, lives improved, because someone cared ... do what you can to show you care about other people, and you will make our world a better place."

– Rosalynn Carter, first lady of the United States from 1977 to 1981

GLOSSARY

altruism. A motivational state with the ultimate goal of increasing another's welfare.

apathy. A lack of interest or concern, closely related to deliberate indifference.

appropriate action. The method of identifying what to do when verbal conflict management methods don't work, or a clearly articulable safety violation exists.

be alert & decisive. The method of being aware of your surroundings and ready to take appropriate action if needed or required.

beyond active listening. The method of advanced listening to gather information, enable perspective-taking, show respect, and demonstrate concern.

bystander effect. Phenomenon in which someone is less likely to intervene in an emergency when others are present than when they are alone.

bystander intervention. Recognizing a potentially harmful situation or interaction and choosing to respond in a way that could positively influence the outcome.

closure. The method for ending interactions safely and on a positive note.

communication alignment. When all of your proxemics (distance), non-verbals (expressions and other body language), verbals (word choices), and para-verbals (tone and volume of voice) are in agreement with your intended message. If you intend to show empathy, but your facial expression shows irritation, it won't matter how sincerely you try to deliver your words.

complicity. Being involved with others in illegal activity or wrongdoing, through actions, planning, enabling, encouraging, or omitting to take action to prevent or stop it.

conformity. The process by which your beliefs or behaviors are influenced by others. People can be influenced via subtle or even unconscious processes or by direct and overt peer pressure. Group behavior, including factors such as group size, unanimity, cohesion, status, prior commitment, and public opinion, helps to determine the level of conformity an individual will reflect toward their group.

continuum of care. A care and intervention structure that integrates and includes the organization or community at every level.

core principle. The Vistelar core philosophy of treating people with dignity by showing respect, even if you disagree and regardless of the circumstances.

crisis management. The method to stay safe and promote recovery when interacting with individuals having cognitive challenges and exhibiting at-risk behaviors.

defamation of character. The act of making untrue statements about another that damages their reputation. If the defamatory statement is printed or broadcast through the media, it is libel. If only oral, it is slander.

defensive atmosphere. An environment by which employees feel emotionally, physically, or psychological threatened and enter a defensive state of being.

diffusion of responsibility. Phenomenon whereby each bystander's sense of responsibility to help decreases as the number of witnesses increases.

discrimination. Differential treatment based on unfair categorization. It is a denial of fairness prompted by prejudice, compassion fatigue, and desensitization.

domestic violence. Acts of physical, sexual, psychological, and social violence that occur as part of familial and personal relationships, such as intimate partner abuse, child abuse, elder abuse, and abuse of disabled family members.

empathy. The ability to experience events/emotions the way another person experiences them.

ethical intervention. A process of intrusion into value systems (ethically) based on a relationship of mutual trust and shared expectations between the intervener and the participant.

gateway behaviors of violence. Antisocial behaviors that may or may not make a person feel threatened at the moment but have been shown to be reliable predictors of violence, such as shouting, cursing, name-calling, or aggressive posturing.

group think. A type of thought exhibited by group members who try to minimize conflict and reach consensus without critically testing, analyzing, and evaluating ideas.

harassment. Threats or other conduct that in any way create a hostile environment, impair organizational operations, or frighten, alarm, or inhibit others.

informational conformity. When in an ambiguous or unclear situation, one turns to their own in-group to determine socially acceptable behaviors.

injury to reputation. A claim that an individual or organization suffered loss as a result of what you said about them; reputation harm.

lateral violence. non-physical, but harmful, behavior between members of a community. While individual acts of lateral violence can appear relatively harmless, they ultimately create a toxic environment that takes a toll on employee morale, hindering the success of the agencies for which they work.

normative conformity. When one conforms to be liked or accepted by the members of the group.

perspective-taking. Reflects a tendency to use one's existing role-taking capacities to entertain the psychological point of view of another person.

persuasion. The method to achieve cooperation while de-escalating the situation, avoiding escalation, and if necessary, confirming non-compliance.

physical assault. To touch another person without explicit or implicit permission or with the intent to cause physical or emotional harm.

pluralistic ignorance. Phenomenon whereby bystanders assume that nothing is wrong in an emergency because no one else looks concerned. This greatly interferes with the interpretation of the event as a problem/emergency and therefore reduces helping.

precision of word choice. The reminder to be mindful that even a slight change of word choice can drastically change the meaning and impact of an intended message. Words mean very different things to different people as a result of cultural expectations, assumptions, and biases.

prejudice. An attitude, opinion, or belief, often guiding decision making and made or held without adequate prior knowledge, thought, or reason.

professional intervention. A professional duty to intervene when we witness others heading in a direction or taking inappropriate action. This includes the duty to assist, fix, stop, and report the event appropriately.

prosocial behavior. Any act performed to benefit another person.

proxemics 10-5-2. The method to enhance your personal safety, display respect, and not cause discomfort in the other person.

redirection. The method to de-escalate verbal resistance and get back to the issue at hand/professional outcome goal.

respond, don't react. The method to minimize the chance that your behavior will escalate a situation.

showtime mindset. The method to become emotionally, mentally, and physically prepared to respond appropriately to any situation.

social contract. An implicit or explicit agreement of expected behavior, obligations, and privileges among the members of a group.

social norms theory. Individuals incorrectly perceive the attitudes and/or behaviors of peers and other community members.

spiral of silence. A theory that asserts a person is less likely to voice an opinion if one feels they are in the minority for fear of reprisal or isolation from the majority.

stalking. Repeated and unwanted interference with the freedom of another person, which places that person in reasonable fear of professional, social, psychological, and/or bodily harm or death.

stereotype. An oversimplified generalization about a person or a group of people without regard for individual differences.

supportive atmosphere. Employees will not be able to talk through anything effectively if they feel threatened in any way and/or enter a defensive state of being. Create an environment by which they feel comfortable and supported by being authentic, sincere, and empathetic.

threat. Any written or oral expression or physical gesture or action that could be reasonably interpreted as conveying an intent to cause harm to persons or property.

transcend the "isms." Acknowledging and moving beyond personal assumptions and beliefs of racism, classism, sexism, heterosexism, ableism, and ageism to find respectful and common ground (in-group inclusivity).

universal greeting. The method for initiating contact that fosters collaboration and minimizes the chance of escalation.

value-based decisions. A cost-benefit analysis where the total value of the chosen behavior is better than the alternative choice.

verbal assault. To attack another person via spoken or written words with the intent to cause emotional pain, social injury, or damage to personal or professional reputation.

workplace violence responder. An individual who has an explicit duty to assist in the prevention, response, mitigation, and recovery from gateway behaviors, threats, violence, or potentially violent situations (e.g., security officers, safety managers, human resource managers, law enforcement officers).

REFERENCES & RESOURCES

Ayakdaş D. & Arslantaş, H. (2018). Colleague violence in nursing: A cross-sectional study. *Journal of Psychiatric Nursing*, 9(1), 36-44.

Bambi, S., Foà, C., De Felippis, C., Lucchini, A., Guazzini, A., & Rasero, L. (2018). Workplace incivility, lateral violence and bullying among nurses. A review about their prevalence and related factors. *Acta biomedica: Atenei Parmensis*, 89(6-S), 51–79. https://doi.org/10.23750/abm.v89i6-S.7461

Carlson, S.M., Cowart, M.E. & Speake, D.L. (1992). Causes of the nursing shortage: A critical review of the theoretical and empirical literature. *Journal of Health Human Resource Administration*, 15(2), 224-250.

De Becker, G. (1999). *The Gift of Fear and Other Survival Signals that Protect Us from Violence*. Dell.

Dovidio, J.F., Piliavin, J.A., Schroeder, D.A., & Penner, L.A. (2006). *The Social Psychology of Prosocial Behavior (1st ed.)*. Psychology Press.

Edwards, R., Thurman, P., Plested, B., Oetting, E.R. & Swanson, L. (2000). The Community Readiness Model: Research to Practice. *Journal of Community Psychology*, 28.

Elgin, S.H. (2000). *The Gentle Art of Verbal Self-Defense at Work*. Prentice Hall.

Elmblad R., Kodjebacheva G. & Lebeck, L. (2014). Workplace incivility affecting CRNAs: A study of prevalence, severity, and consequences with proposed interventions. *AANA Journal*, 82, 437-45.

Englander, E.K. & Raffalli, P. (2012). Physicians Can Address, Prevent Bullying Behaviors. *Family Practice News*, 01/2012; 42(1), 21-23. DOI:1

Fehr, B.J., & Exline, R.V. (1987). Social visual interactions: A conceptual and literature review. A.W. Siegman & S. Feldstein (Editors), Nonverbal Behavior and Communication, *Psychology Press*, 225-326.

Frank, M.G. & Eckman, P. (1997). The ability to detect deceit generalizes across different types of high-stake lies. *Journal of Personality and Social Psychology*, 72, 1429-1439.

Gilmartin, K.M. (2002). *Emotional survival for law enforcement: A guide for officers and their families*. E-S Press.

Grossman, D. (2009). *On Killing: The Psychological Cost of Learning to Kill in War and Society*. Back Bay Books.

Hall, E.T. (1963). A system for the notation of proxemic behaviors. *American Anthropologist*, 65, 1003-1026.

Henderson, A. (2003). Nurses and Workplace Violence: Nurses' Experiences of Verbal and Physical Abuse at Work. *Nursing Leadership*, 16, 82-98. 10.12927/cjnl.2003.16263.

Hoban, J.E. (2012). *The Ethical Warrior: Values, Morals and Ethics - For Life, Work and Service*. CreateSpace.

Hoel, H., & Cooper, C.L. (2000). *Destructive Conflict & Bullying at Work*. Manchester School of Management, University of Manchester, Institute of Science and Technology.

Horn, S. (1997). *Tongue Fu!: How to Deflect, Disarm, and Defuse Any Verbal Conflict*. St. Martin's Griffin.

Hortensius, R. & de Gelder, B. (2018). From Empathy to Apathy: The Bystander Effect Revisited. *Current Directions in Psychological Science*, 27(4), 249-256.

Huntington, B., & Kuhn, N. (2003). Communication gaffes: A root cause of malpractice claims. *Baylor University Medical Centre Proceedings*, 16(2), 157-161.

Katz, N.H. et al. (1992). *Communication & Conflict Resolution Skills*. Kendall Hunt Publishing.

Klugiewicz, G. et al. (2016). *Conflict Management for Law Enforcement*. Truths Publishing.

Knapp, M.L. & Hall, J.A. (2013). *Nonverbal Communication in Human Interaction*. Wadsworth Publishing.

Latané, B. & Darley, J.M. (1970). *The unresponsive bystander: Why doesn't he help?*. Appleton Century Crofts.

Lashley, J. (2015). *Confidence in Conflict for Healthcare Professionals: Creating an Environment of Care that is Incompatible with Violence*. Truths Publishing.

Leiter M.P., Price, S.L. & Spence Laschinger, H.K. (2010). Generational differences in distress, attitudes and incivility among nurses. *Journal of Nursing Management*, 18, 970-80.

Matsumoto, D., Frank, M.G. & Hwang, H. S. (2012). *Nonverbal Communication: Science and Applications*. Sage Publications Inc.

Mattice, C.M. & Garman, K. (2010). *Proactive Solutions for Workplace Bullying: Looking at the Benefits of Positive Psychology*. Paper to be presented at the International Association for Workplace Bullying & Harassment, Cardiff, Wales.

Modell, D. (2013). *"The Psychology of the Active Killer."* Law Enforcement Executive Forum, 13(4). Retrieved 2021-03-11 – via Ares Tactics.

Morrison, M.F., Lindo, J.M.L., Aiken, J. & Chin, C.R. (2017). Lateral violence among nurses at a Jamaican hospital: A mixed methods study. *International Journal of Africa Nursing Sciences*, 6(2), 85-91.

Oyeleye, O., Hanson, P., O'Connor, N. & Dunn, D. (2013). Relationship of workplace incivility, stress, and burnout on nurses' turnover intentions and psychological empowerment. *Journal of Nursing Administration*, 43, 536-42.

Pearson, C. & Porath, C. (2009). *The Cost of Bad Behavior: How Incivility is Damaging Your Business and What to Do About it.* Portfolio Hardcover.

Porath, C. & Pearson, C. (2012). Emotional and Behavioral Responses to Workplace Incivility and the Impact of Hierarchical Status. *Journal of Applied Social Psychology*, 42. 10.1111/j.1559-1816.2012.01020.x.

Porath, C. & Pearson, C. (2013). The price of incivility. *Harvard Business Review, Jan-Feb*, 91(1-2),114-21, 146. PMID: 23390745.

Reitz, M. & Higgins, J. (2019). *Speak Up: Say what needs to be said and hear what news to be heard.* FT Publishing International.

Reitz, M. & Higgins, J. (2020). *Speaking Truth to Power: Why Leaders Cannot Hear What They Need To Hear.* British Medical Journal Leader.

Remsberg, C. et al. (1987). *Street Survival: Tactics for Armed Encounters.* Calibre Press.

Smith, L.M., Andrusyszyn, M.A. & Spence Laschinger, H.K. (2010). Effects of workplace incivility and empowerment on newly graduated nurses' organizational commitment. *Journal of Nursing Management*, 18, 1004-15.

Spence Laschinger, H.K., Leiter, M., Day, A. & Gilin, D. (2009). Workplace empowerment, incivility, and burnout: Impact on staff nurse recruitment and retention outcomes. *Journal of Nursing Management*, 17, 302-11.

Sull, D. & Sull, C. (2021). *10 Things Your Corporate Culture Needs to Get Right*. MIT Sloan Management Review.

Sull, D., Sull, C., & Zweig, B (2022). *Toxic Culture is Driving the Great Resignation*. MIT Sloan Management Review.

Sutton, R.I. (2007). *The No Asshole Rule. Building a Civilized Workplace and Surviving One That Isn't*. Warner Business Books.

Topa, G. & Moriano, J.A. (2013). Stress and nurses' horizontal mobbing: Moderating effects of group identity and group support. *Nursing Outlook*, 61, 25-31.

Van Horn, P. & Riley J.A. (2014). *Left of Bang: How the Marine Corps' Combat Hunter Program Can Save Your Life*. Black Irish Entertainment LLC, Illustrated edition.

Vartia MA-L. Consequences of workplace bullying with respect to the well-being of its targets and the observers of bullying. *Scand J Work Environ Health*. 2001;27(1):63–69. doi:10.5271/sjweh.5588.

Weisensel, J. (2014). *Confidence in Conflict for Campus Life: The Must-Have Safety Resource for Every College and College-Bound Student*. Truths Publishing.

Young, D. (2017). *How to Defend Your Family and Home: Outsmart an Invader, Secure Your Home, Prevent a Burglary and Protect Your Loved Ones from Any Threat*. Page Street Publishing.

Young, D. (2018). Surviving as a Hostage. *Police Magazine*, 42(9).

Jill Weisensel

BENEFITS

After reading this book, the reader will have the knowledge, skills, and abilities to be the first line of defense to reduce workplace violence.

This book aims to increase safety and improve outcomes in these four areas (P.O.L.E.):

Physical: Improved threat assessment and violence prevention.

Organizational: Improved job performance, morale, and collaboration.

Legal: Protection from personal liability, career pitfalls, and damaged reputation.

Emotional: Improved relationships, self-confidence, and quality of life.

As this information becomes part of your organizational culture, the results will include:

- Enhanced client satisfaction and outcomes.

- Decreased risk and liability.

- Increased safety for workers and their clients.

- Increased worker performance and morale.

- More effective service recovery and complaint resolution.
- Less absenteeism and increased retention.
- Fewer worker compensation claims.

ABOUT THE AUTHOR

Jill Weisensel is the Instructional Design Lead for Vistelar LLC, an internationally known conflict management solution straining company that helps organizations build safe and respectful workplaces that addresses the entire spectrum of violence. She has over 20 years of experience working in hospital security, law enforcement, and education.

She is the author of *Confidence in Conflict for Campus Life* (Truths Publishing, 2014), a verbal de-escalation and personal safety book written for high school students preparing for college life. She is also the co-developer of the TAKES ACTION bystander intervention program, developed during her time at Marquette University, which spurred her interest in the need for ethical intervention in professional settings.

In addition to speaking at multiple Midwest colleges, high schools, and corporate training events, she has presented her research and training philosophy at numerous state and national conferences, including the Association of Wisconsin School Administrators Principle's Conference, the Big Brothers Big Sisters Regional Conference, Boys and Girls Clubs of Milwaukee Sexual Violence Prevention events, and the 2014 National Association of Student Personnel Administrators (NASPA) National Conference. Most notably, she presented her work at the 2015 International Association of Chiefs of Police International Conference, and the International Association of Campus Law Enforcement Administrators National Conferences in 2015, 2017, 2018, and 2019.

Her academic background (she earned her Master's degree in Kinesiology with an emphasis in Sports Psychology from the University of Wisconsin - Milwaukee, and her Bachelor's degree in Criminal Justice and Sociology from Carthage College), athletic training and professional experience make her uniquely qualified to address topics in teaching and speaking such as: personal safety and self-defense, the need for personal credibility and professional development, and the development of leadership and life skills. She holds the designation of Certified Public Manager from the University of Wisconsin - Madison, and lives by the mantra that the truly educated never graduate.

ACKNOWLEDGEMENTS

The topic of lateral violence is not an easy one for me.

In fact. It hurts.

I have painfully lived through, worked through, and led through pretty much every example in this book–always trying to find "a better way" to treat people, respect people, and lead.

I've always said, "If you're not a part of the solution, you very well could be a part of the problem." And I believe that, wholeheartedly, as I've always worked towards solutions. I mean, leadership is a verb, after all–isn't it?

I imagine that the topics of lateral violence, workplace violence, and workplace toxicity are not comfortable for many of you, either. For that reason, I commend you for both your curiosity and courage in looking for a solution.

So, thank you, truly. Thank you for picking up this book and reading it. We all have a role to play in creating environments that are incompatible with emotional and physical violence, and I truly believe that this book will help all of us do better.

With that being said, there are a few thank yous in order:

- To the people along the way who have taught me "what not to do," thank you for the perspective.

- To the people along the way who have taught me what it means to be a leader, thank you for allowing me to stand on the shoulders of giants.

- To the entire Vistelar team, thank you for your vision and support. Without you, this book would not have been possible.

- To Joel Lashley, thank you for your infinite insight and wisdom on this topic. The world needs more people who think like you.

- To Jen Tucker, you are a fantastic editor and thought leader. Thank you for your expertise and incredible ability to consolidate my thoughts, even when I couldn't.

- To Heather Keenan and John Konecny, thank you for your inspiring design work.

- To my family and friends, and my friends who are family, thank you. Thank you for supporting me and standing by me, even through the thickest of times.

- And finally, to my other half, you inspire me to be a better person every day. Thank you for being you, and for being with me every step of the way.

WHO IS VISTELAR

Throughout this book, there are numerous references to a company called Vistelar. I have been actively engaged with this company since 2010 and am now a partner/owner.

Vistelar is a licensing, training, and consulting institute focused on helping organizations build safe and respectful workplaces via verbal and physical conflict management solutions. We empower teams to safely and effectively identify, prevent, and mitigate all types of conflict, from simple disputes to physical violence. Our training is delivered using online, virtual, and onsite methods of instruction.

I am one of a small group of contributors to the Vistelar *Unified Conflict Management System* that addresses the entire spectrum of human conflict and that emphasizes simplicity and universal application with all tactics taught. This system is the outcome of over four decades of research and real-world experience and I'm proud to have been involved in its development.

We work with such disciplines as healthcare, behavioral health, education, security, social services, home visitation, hospitality, customer service, transit, and law enforcement. We train contact professionals — individuals who spend the vast majority of their time directly interacting with the general public or their organization's clients — and organizational teams impacted by workplace and/or lateral violence.

Vistelar currently offers the following training programs:

- Non-Escalation, De-Escalation, and Crisis Management
- Cognitive Challenges
- Personal Protection and Safety
- Personal Safety For Home Visit Workers
- Positive Interventions and Stabilization
- Workplace Violence Prevention and Intervention
  - Lateral Violence
  - Behavioral Emergency Response Team
  - Active Shooter
- Healthcare Workplace Violence Prevention and Intervention
  - Team Response to Emergencies
- Physical Alternatives — P.O.S.C.®

The content of this book is largely based on the *Non-Escalation, De-Escalation, and Crisis Management* and *Lateral Violence* training programs. For readers of this book, an online resource is available that provides some additional training beyond the content of this book. You can access this resource at:

www.endinglateralviolence.com

Made in USA - Kendallville, IN
56958_9781732376816
07.24.2023 1319